HOLY COW,

CHICAGO'S COOKING!

A choice collection of recipes
seasoned with a dash of Chicago history

The Church of the Holy Comforter
Kenilworth, Illinois

First Edition

First Printing, August 1993

© Copyright 1993
The Church of the Holy Comforter
Kenilworth, Illinois
All Rights Reserved

ISBN 0-9632548-0-4
LCCN 93-71359

The profit realized by the sale of
Holy Cow, Chicago's Cooking!
will provide outreach assistance to
organizations in the metropolitan
Chicago area by focusing on issues
such as hunger, education,
homelessness, and families at risk.

For your convenience, order blanks
are included in the back of this book.

Printed on recycled paper

Printed in the USA by
WIMMER
The Wimmer Companies, Inc.
Memphis • Dallas

LEGENDS of Chicago abound but none is more enduring than that of Mrs. O'Leary, her cow, and the great Chicago Fire.

CHICAGO in October of 1871 had suffered through three months without rain. The city was dry as a tinderbox and small fires had been springing up spontaneously. All of these had been successfully extinguished until the night of October 8, 1871, when Mrs. O'Leary, a boarding housekeeper on DeKoven Street, went to the barn to milk her cow.

FOLKLORE tells us that Mrs. O'Leary left a lighted lantern in the barn when she finished milking and her cow kicked over the lantern igniting straw in the stall. The fire, fanned by a southwest wind, spread throughout the business district and destroyed much of the North Side of Chicago until it was contained by Lake Michigan and a heavy rain shower. Among those buildings in the fire's path, only the pumping station of the Chicago Water Company remained standing.

THE FIRE raged for thirty-six hours but within hours after the end of the blaze, the city had begun to rebuild. Mrs. O'Leary and her cow are indeed a part of urban legend and the reconstruction of the city after the Great Fire has led to the magnificent Chicago skyline which we admire today.

The Church of the Holy Comforter was
established in 1898, and became a parish of the
Episcopal Church in 1902. Today, Holy Comforter
is the Christian community of some 300 families.

TABLE OF CONTENTS

Drawings by Gretchen Grant
Design by Courtney Boyd Davis

Both artists are members of the parish,
Church of the Holy Comforter, Kenilworth, Illinois.

APPETIZERS and BEVERAGES

Mrs. O'Leary milks her famous cow!

APPETIZERS

BEVERAGES

TROUT CEVICHE

2 pounds ocean trout, cut
into 1-inch squares
2 cups fresh lime juice
1 teaspoon salt
3 tablespoons chopped
jalapeño peppers
2 medium diced tomatoes
1 medium diced onion

4 tablespoons white wine
4 tablespoons olive oil
10 green onions, chopped
¼ teaspoon soy sauce
½ teaspoon Worcestershire
sauce
1 teaspoon salt
1 teaspoon dill

Marinate fish in lime juice and 1 teaspoon salt for 3 to 4 hours. Rinse
in colander. Mix remaining ingredients in large mixing bowl. Add
fish. Cover and refrigerate overnight. Serve with crackers, tostada
chips or as a small salad.

Yield: 2½ cups

PESTO PINWHEELS

12 ounces cream cheese
½ cup grated Parmesan
cheese
½ cup grated imported
Romano cheese

3 small green onions, cut in
1-inch pieces
¾ cup pesto sauce, drained
of surface oil
1 pound frozen puff pastry
dough, thawed

In a food processor or blender, combine cheeses and green onions
until smooth. Add pesto; mix well. Unroll one sheet of puff pastry
and roll to extend the length to 16 inches. Spread ½ the mixture
over the pastry, bringing it to the edges. Starting at the long side, roll
up into a tight cylinder. Repeat with remaining dough and mixture.
Wrap in plastic wrap and freeze at least 2 hours or as long as a month.
Heat oven to 400°. Unwrap cylinders. With a sharp serrated knife,
cut into ¼-inch slices. If the cylinders are too difficult to slice, let
stand for 15 to 20 minutes. Arrange on ungreased baking sheets.
Bake until golden (about 10 minutes). Serve warm.

Yield: approximately 70 appetizers

GOAT CHEESE BAGUETTE

1 thin baguette	¼ cup olive oil
8 ounces goat cheese	1 cup freshly grated
4 plum tomatoes	Parmesan cheese
4 ounces fresh basil, chopped	

Cut baguette, goat cheese and tomatoes into 24 ¼-inch slices. Lightly toast bread slices. Arrange the bread in a single layer on a platter. Brush each piece with olive oil. Place one piece of cheese on each piece of bread. Overlap the cheese with a slice of tomato. Sprinkle the basil and Parmesan cheese over the bread slices.

Yield: 24 appetizers

ONIONS WITH SAUSAGE STUFFING

6 small onions, about 1½-inch in diameter	1 egg
½ pound Italian sausage, removed from its casing	1 tablespoon dried Italian herbs
½ cup bread crumbs	1 cup beef stock
½ cup dry white wine or vermouth	salt and pepper to taste
	fennel ferns to garnish

In a small saucepan, parboil the onions in water to cover (about 10 minutes). Do not overcook. Cut off the root ends flat and separate into little domes. They should be about 2 layers thick; and about 3 domes per onion. Finely chop the remaining onion centers and sauté with the Italian sausage until cooked through. Add bread crumbs, wine, egg and seasonings. Salt and pepper to taste. Stuff onion domes from the bottom, being careful to pack them without splitting the onion skin. Place in a flat-bottomed baking dish which just holds all the onions placed close together, points up. Pour beef stock around the domes and bake at 300° until just poached, about ½ hour. Cool. Remove from the stock and store in a flat, covered dish in the refrigerator. Serve at room temperature. Garnish with fennel ferns and serve.

Yield: 18 to 20 appetizers

PARSNIP CHIPS

4 slices bacon	1 cup vegetable oil
4 large peeled parsnips	salt to taste

Cook bacon until very crisp, then crumble into small bits. Using a vegetable peeler, shave the parsnips into long, thin strips. Work from two sides, discarding the inner core. Heat oil in a deep fryer or heavy saucepan. Shake in a handful of parsnips; do not crowd. Fry until crisp and golden. Remove with a slotted spoon and drain on paper towels. Salt lightly. Repeat with remaining parsnips. Pile the parsnips on a serving dish and sprinkle with the bacon bits. Serve as an appetizer or side dish.

Yield: 48

CRAB AND BRIE APPETIZER

8 ounce wheel of Brie cheese	1 clove garlic, crushed
½ cup butter or margarine	¼ teaspoon dried basil
2 tablespoons minced parsley	8 ounces crab meat
	1 14 to 16-inch loaf French bread

Remove rind from cheese; cut cheese into chunks. In medium saucepan, melt butter, add cheese, parsley, garlic and basil. Cook over medium heat until blended, stirring often. Fold in crab meat and remove from heat. Cut bread in half lengthwise; spread with crab mixture. Place on baking sheet. Broil 6 inches from heat for 5 minutes or until bubbly. Cut into wedges and serve. May be prepared up to 24 hours in advance before broiling.

Yield: 2 to 2½ dozen 1-inch appetizers

HERB GARLIC CHEESE

1 (8-ounce) package cream cheese
½ stick of butter (not margarine)
½ teaspoon Beau Monde seasoning
1 medium clove garlic, pressed
¼ teaspoon herbs de Provence
1 teaspoon water
1 teaspoon fresh parsley (if using dried, moisten in the 1 tablespoon water before including)
¼ teaspoon red wine vinegar
¼ teaspoon Worcestershire sauce

Cream together butter and cheese until fluffy. Add the remaining ingredients. Serve with crackers or stuff in endive. If frozen, defrost and beat until smooth.

Yield: 1 cup

CHUTNEY PÂTÉ

6 ounces softened cream cheese
1 cup shredded Cheddar cheese
1 tablespoon dry sherry
¾ teaspoon curry powder
¼ teaspoon salt
    dash pepper sauce
½ cup chutney
3 chopped green onions
¼ cup chopped peanuts to garnish

In a blender or food processor, beat cream and Cheddar cheese until smooth. Add sherry, curry, salt and pepper sauce. Spread on a serving plate in a circle. Top with chutney, green onions and peanuts if desired. Serve with crackers.

Yield: 6 to 8 servings

BASIL CHEESE PÂTÉ

1 (8-ounce) package
  softened cream cheese
4 ounces Roquefort cheese,
  at room temperature
1 cup loosely packed,
  chopped Swiss chard
½ cup loosely packed, fresh
  parsley
¼ cup loosely packed fresh
  basil

1 teaspoon minced garlic
¼ cup vegetable oil
¼ cup finely chopped
  walnuts or pecans
1 cup freshly grated
  Parmesan cheese
¼ cup slivered sun-dried
  tomatoes

Combine the cream cheese and Roquefort in a bowl. Mix until smooth; set aside. Combine the Swiss chard, parsley, basil and garlic in the bowl of a food processor or blender. With the motor running, slowly drizzle the oil through the feed tube. Continue processing or blending until smooth. Transfer the mixture to a bowl. Add walnuts or pecans, Parmesan cheese and mix thoroughly. Line a 5½ x 2½-inch loaf pan with plastic wrap, leaving extra wrap hanging over the sides. Spread ⅓ of the cheese mixture evenly over the bottom of the pan. Over that, spread ½ of the Swiss Chard mixture and arrange a layer of sun-dried tomatoes on top. Repeat. Finish with the remaining ⅓ of the cheese mixture. Cover with the overhanging plastic wrap and refrigerate for 24 hours. To serve, allow the loaf to warm to room temperature. Invert it onto a platter and provide a cheese spreader. Serve with crackers or bread.

Yield: 6 to 8 servings

FORGET THE CHOLESTEROL PÂTÉ

1½ cups chopped green
onions, including stems
2½ sticks unsalted butter
1 pound trimmed chicken
livers
1 pound fresh cleaned
mushrooms, including
stems

6 quartered hard-boiled
eggs
¼ cups fresh lemon juice
1 teaspoon salt
1 teaspoon fresh ground
black pepper
1 teaspoon cayenne pepper
1 cup dry bread crumbs

In a large skillet, gently sauté the green onions approximately 5 minutes in butter until clear. Purée the chicken livers, mushrooms and eggs in blender or food processor. Add chicken liver mixture to the onions and butter; cook over low heat stirring constantly for about 5 minutes or until livers are not pink. Transfer to a large mixing bowl. Add lemon juice and seasonings; stir well. Add enough bread crumbs to bind the mixture. It should begin to form a ball and stick together. Place in lightly greased springform pan and refrigerate for 4 hours. Serve with party-size rye and pumpernickel slices or whole wheat crackers. This may be prepared up to 3 days before serving.

Yield: 8 cups

GREEN PEPPERCORN PÂTÉ

6 tablespoons sweet butter	2 teaspoons dry sherry
½ cup finely chopped onion	½ teaspoon salt
2 cloves garlic, chopped	½ teaspoon ground allspice
1 teaspoon dried thyme	½ cup heavy cream
½ cup celery tops	5 teaspoons water-packed
10 black peppercorns	green peppercorns,
2 bay leaves	drained
6 cups water	fresh parsley or chervil
1 pound chicken livers	to garnish

Melt butter in a skillet. Add the onion, garlic and thyme; cook, covered, over medium heat 2 to 5 minutes until onion is tender and lightly colored. Add celery tops, peppercorns and bay leaves to 6 cups of water in a saucepan. Bring to boil, reduce heat, simmer 10 minutes. Add chicken livers to water. Simmer gently for about 10 minutes; livers should be slightly pink inside. Drain livers, discard celery tops, bay leaves and peppercorns. Place livers, butter, onion and garlic in the bowl of a food processor fitted with a steel blade. Add sherry, salt, pepper, allspice and 4 teaspoons green peppercorns. Process until smooth. Pour in cream. Process again to blend. Transfer to a bowl; stir in remaining teaspoon of green peppercorns. Scrape mixture into a 2-cup terrine. Cover and refrigerate for at least 4 hours before serving. Let pâté stand at room temperature before serving. Garnish with parsley or chervil. Serve with crackers or baguettes.

Yield: 8 servings

SALMON CHEESE CAKE

¼ cup bread crumbs, toasted
⅛ cup grated Gruyère cheese
¼ teaspoon dried dill
3 tablespoons margarine
1 medium onion, finely chopped

2 (8-ounce) packages cream cheese, softened
4 eggs
½ cup grated Gruyère cheese
⅓ cup half-and-half
½ pound smoked salmon, chopped

Mix bread crumbs, ⅛ cup Gruyère cheese and dill. Grease a 9-inch springform pan. Add crumbs to pan, covering bottom and sides. Sauté onion in margarine until translucent. In a food processor, blend cream cheese until smooth. Add eggs, ½ cup Gruyère cheese and half-and-half. Add onion and salmon; mixture should be lumpy. Pour into prepared pan. Set pan in a larger pan filled with water to come ½-inch up the sides of the springform pan. Bake at 325° for 1 hour 20 minutes. Cool. Serve with a variety of crackers.

Yield: 12 servings

SMOKED SALMON MOUSSE

8 tablespoons butter
½ pound smoked salmon
salt and pepper
1 tablespoon lemon juice

1 tablespoon chopped fresh chervil or dill
⅔ cup heavy cream
cucumber slices to garnish

Melt the butter in a small saucepan. Cool slightly. Place salmon, lemon juice, chervil and cream in food processor. With the machine running, pour in the melted butter and process until smooth. Season with salt and pepper. Spoon the pâté into a serving dish and garnish with slices of cucumber. Serve with melba toast or crackers.

Yield: 8 servings

CAJUN MUSHROOMS

2	pounds medium-sized mushrooms	1	teaspoon salt
1	pound Andouille sausage	4	tablespoons butter
1	large onion, finely chopped	1	cup fresh bread crumbs
2	large cloves garlic	½	cup freshly grated Parmesan cheese

Remove stems from mushrooms. Finely chop ½ of stems. Remaining stems may be discarded. Place mushroom caps on a cookie sheet. Sauté stems, sausage, onion, garlic and salt in butter until sausage is brown; drain fat. Add bread crumbs and cheese. Stuff caps with mixture. Broil for 2 to 5 minutes. Serve immediately.

Yield: 36 mushroom caps

CLAM STUFFED MUSHROOMS

1	(8-ounce) package cream cheese	½	teaspoon horseradish
1	(6.5 ounce) can minced clams, reserve liquid	¼	teaspoon salt
			dash pepper
2	tablespoons finely chopped onion	1	tablespoon milk
		30	large mushrooms
½	teaspoon dill	8	tablespoons butter
		½	teaspoon minced garlic

In a large mixing bowl, blend together all ingredients except mushrooms, garlic and butter; set aside. Remove stems from mushrooms and finely chop. Sauté stems in 4 tablespoons butter with the garlic. Mix in with rest of mixture. In a medium sized skillet, melt 4 tablespoons butter. Dip caps in butter. Stuff with mixture. Place on a cookie sheet and bake for 20 minutes in a 375° oven.

Yield: 30 mushroom caps

ARUGULA WATERCRESS CANAPES

½ bunch fresh arugula
½ bunch fresh watercress
½ small white onion
   dash of hot pepper sauce
   salt to taste
1 tablespoon lemon juice

2 tablespoons good
   mayonnaise
4 slices firm white bread
   red or yellow pepper
   (optional)

Rinse arugula and watercress stems; pat dry. Remove coarse stems and make sure there is no excess moisture. Finely chop arugula, watercress and onion by hand or in a food processor. Add remaining ingredients except bread. Reserve mixture. Toast bread. While still warm, cut 4 rounds from each slice with 1½-inch biscuit cutter. Spread rounds on a rack to keep them from becoming soggy. Store in an airtight container. At serving time, using a teaspoon, mound the filling on the toast rounds covering to the edge. Garnish with red or yellow pepper. If arugula cannot be found, may use all watercress.

Yield: 12 to 16 canapes

CHINESE NACHOS

1 cup plum jelly
½ cup mango chutney
1½ tablespoons red wine
   vinegar
1 teaspoon dry mustard
¼ teaspoon hot pepper
   sauce

1 (14-ounce) package
   won ton skins
   vegetable oil
   chopped green onions
   to garnish

Combine jelly, chutney, vinegar, mustard and hot pepper sauce in a heavy small saucepan. Stir over medium heat until thoroughly blended and bubbly. Cut won tons in half diagonally. Heat oil in deep fryer or skillet to 365°. Add won tons in small batches and fry until golden brown; approximately 2 minutes. Drain on paper towels. Spoon sauce into bowl. Garnish with green onions. Serve hot or at room temperature surrounded by fried won tons.

Yield: 6 to 8 servings

CHEESE PRETZELS

1 cup all-purpose flour	½ teaspoon garlic powder
½ cup butter or margarine	½ teaspoon onion powder
2 tablespoons grated Parmesan cheese	1 teaspoon Italian herbs
	3 to 3½ teaspoons water
1 cup shredded sharp Cheddar cheese	

Combine flour and butter. With a pastry blender or 2 knives, cut in the butter until particles are no longer distinguishable. Stir in Parmesan and Cheddar cheeses, garlic and onion powder, and herbs. Sprinkle the water over the mixture, a tablespoon at a time, while you toss it lightly with a fork until moistened. Gather dough up into a ball. Divide in ½, then divide each portion into 12 equal pieces. If dough seems too soft, wrap in wax paper and chill until firm. Roll pieces of dough with your palms on a very lightly floured board into thin, 11-inch ropes. Twist into pretzel shapes; place slightly apart on ungreased baking sheets. Bake in a 425° oven for 12 to 15 minutes or until golden. Cool on wire racks. Wrap airtight and freeze if made ahead. Recrisp, without thawing, on baking sheets in a 350° oven for 5 to 7 minutes.

Yield: 2 dozen

CHEESE CRISPS

½ cup butter	¼ teaspoon cayenne pepper
10 ounces sharp Cheddar cheese	1 to 2 teaspoons fennel seed
2 ounces Parmesan cheese	½ teaspoon salt

Put all ingredients in a food processor. Process until mixture is completely combined and forms a ball. Shape into long cylinders about 1½ inches in diameter. Wrap in waxed paper. Chill. Cut into ¼-inch slices and place on a cookie sheet lined with parchment paper or brown paper, leaving an inch between the slices. Bake at 350° about 12 to 15 minutes until the crisps are firm. Remove with spatula and store in closed container. When cooled, they may be frozen.

Yield: 4 dozen

RATATOUILLE IN OYSTER CUPS

2 medium zucchini, chopped
1 medium eggplant (1½ pounds), cut into ½-inch cubes
2 red peppers, chopped
2 green peppers, chopped
2 large onions, diced
1 cup olive oil
3 cloves garlic, minced
1 (28-ounce) can tomatoes, undrained
½ cup red wine vinegar
2 tablespoons sugar
3 ounces tomato paste
10 shakes of hot pepper sauce
2 teaspoons salt
½ teaspoon pepper
2 teaspoons dried basil
8 dozen oyster cups
1½ cups grated Parmesan cheese

Shred the zucchini, eggplant, peppers and onion in a food processor or chop by hand. In a large saucepan, combine the olive oil, eggplant, zucchini, peppers, onion, garlic and tomatoes. Cook for 15 minutes. Add the vinegar, sugar, tomato paste, hot pepper sauce, salt, pepper and basil. Cover and simmer for 15 minutes. Cool to room temperature. Fill each oyster cup to the top with cooled ratatouille. Sprinkle with Parmesan cheese. Can be served warm as a vegetable side dish topped with freshly grated Parmesan cheese or served over rice.

Yield: 8 to 10 dozen appetizers, 12 servings as a side dish

SHRIMP-CHEESE PUFFS

½ cup butter, softened
2 cups (8-ounces) shredded Cheddar cheese
1 egg, separated

7 slices bread or 28 slices cocktail rye bread
28 cooked shrimp

Preheat oven to 350°. Cream butter and cheese; blend in egg yolk. Beat egg white until stiff; fold into cheese mixture. Remove crust from bread and cut into quarters. Arrange bread squares on ungreased baking sheet. Top each with a shrimp and cover with rounded teaspoon of cheese mixture. Bake 15 to 18 minutes or until golden brown. To make ahead, assemble, cover and refrigerate up to 12 hours. Bake just before serving.

Yield: 28 pieces

CHILIES RELLENOS

2 (4-ounce) cans diced small green chilies
1 pound grated Cheddar cheese
3 (5-ounce) cans evaporated milk

4 eggs
2 tablespoons flour
2 (8-ounce) cans tomato sauce
1 pound grated Monterey Jack cheese

Preheat oven to 400°. Grease a 13 x 9 x 2-inch glass casserole dish. Place chilies in bottom of casserole. Layer Cheddar cheese on top of chilies. In a blender, mix milk, eggs and flour. Pour over chilies and cheese. Cover and refrigerate overnight. Remove from refrigerator one hour before baking. Bake for 30 minutes. Remove casserole from oven; sprinkle Monterey Jack cheese on top. Pour tomato sauce over the cheese. Bake 15 minutes longer. Cool 15 to 20 minutes before serving. Cut like brownies. May be served as part of a meal or as an appetizer.

Yield: 6 to 12 servings depending on size of pieces

MISSISSIPPI GAMBLER PUNCH

12 lemons, juiced	1 cup sugar
4 cups bourbon whiskey	fresh mint or fresh
4 cups water	parsley for garnish

Squeeze lemons, reserving 8 lemon rinds. Combine lemon juice, whiskey, water and sugar, stirring well. Add the 8 rinds and pour mixture into an old crock or other non-metallic container. After 24 hours squeeze rinds and remove; strain. Allow mixture to mellow for at least 3 days. Two days before serving, place in the freezer. When ready to serve, scoop out iced slush (it will not freeze) into short cocktail glasses. Garnish with fresh sprig of mint or parsley and cocktail straw . May be multiplied for a large party.

Yield: 12 to 16 servings

SPICED TEA

3 tea bags	1 (46-ounce) can pineapple
3 cups water	juice
1 teaspoon whole cloves	½ cup sugar
3 tablespoons fresh lemon juice	

Using a large pot, pour 2 cups of boiling water over 3 tea bags. Steep 5 minutes or until the tea mixture is strong. Add 1 cup of water, cloves, juices and sugar. Let simmer on low at least 20 minutes.

Yield: 12 servings

MULLED CIDER

1 quart apple cider	4 tablespoons brown sugar
1 cup orange juice	1 stick whole cinnamon
2 teaspoons fresh lemon juice	1 teaspoon whole cloves
	½ teaspoon whole allspice

Heat the ingredients in a heavy saucepan. The longer it steeps on a low heat, the more flavorful it becomes. Optional: Add 1 tablespoon of bourbon to each serving of cider.

Yield: 6 servings

CHRISTMAS PUNCH

1 cup water
4 cups sugar
2 tablespoons grated
   nutmeg
3 4-inch sticks cinnamon
2 teaspoons ground ginger

16 whole cloves
12 allspice berries
4 bottles Madeira wine
2 cups brandy
12 washed small red apples

Combine water, sugar, nutmeg, cinnamon, ginger, cloves and all-spice in heavy saucepan and boil for 5 minutes. In separate pan, combine Madeira wine and brandy. Bring almost to a boil. Strain the sugar and spice mixture into a punch bowl, retaining spices and tying in cheesecloth. Place cheesecloth in punch bowl. Pour the wine and brandy over the mixture. Add the apples and serve immediately.

Yield: 24 servings

EGG NOG

18 eggs, separated
1½ cups sugar
1½ pints whipping cream

2 cups milk
¾ cup superfine sugar
1 (750 ml.) bottle dark rum

Beat egg yolks until light. Add sugar, cream and milk. Beat egg whites until stiff. Gradually add sugar, continuing to beat until stiff peaks form. Add rum to egg yolk mixture. Fold in ½ of the egg white mixture until well blended. Place in punch bowl. Top with remaining egg whites, spread evenly over top of mixture. The mixture should touch the sides of the serving bowl sealing the egg nog from the air. Let stand in refrigerator for at least 24 hours before serving. Recipe can be cut in half.

Yield: 26 to 30 servings

BLACKBERRY SPRITZER

1½ cups Chambord (black
    raspberry liqueur)
 8 teaspoons Rose's lime
    juice

½ cup fresh lime juice
6 cups chilled club soda

Divide the Chambord, Rose's lime juice and fresh lime juice evenly among 8 cocktail glasses. Add 2 ice cubes to each glass and fill with club soda.

Yield: 8 servings

GRAPEFRUIT RUM COCKTAIL

1 quart fresh squeezed
  grapefruit juice

8 ounces dark rum
  fresh nutmeg

Mix together grapefruit juice and rum. Pour over ice. Grate fresh nutmeg on top.

Yield: 6 servings

CRANBERRY APRICOT COCKTAIL

3 cups each: ginger ale,
  cranberry juice cocktail
  fresh cranberries
1 (14-ounce) can apricot
  nectar, chilled
2 cups cranberry juice
  cocktail, chilled

¾ cup Cointreau
2 (750 ml.) bottles chilled
  Spanish sparkling wine
  orange slices, lemon
  slices, sprigs fresh mint
  for garnish

Fill an 8-cup ring mold with ginger ale and cranberry juice. Sprinkle very liberally with fresh cranberries and put in freezer overnight. Unmold and set aside for a moment. In a large punch bowl, mix apricot nectar, cranberry juice and Cointreau. Just before serving, pour in the 2 bottles of sparkling wine. Place frozen mold in center of punch. Serve in chilled champagne glasses with a garnish of lemon and orange slices and sprigs of fresh mint.

Yield: 20 ½ cup servings

BREADS

Mrs. O'Leary's house...still standing after the fire!

BREADS

BLUEBERRY MUFFINS

1½ cups all-purpose flour
½ cup sugar
2 tablespoons baking powder
½ teaspoon salt
¼ teaspoon cinnamon

¼ cup soft shortening or softened butter or margarine
1 egg
½ cup milk
¼ cup sherry
¾ cup blueberries

Sift flour, sugar, baking powder, salt and cinnamon together into a mixing bowl. Add softened shortening and mix lightly on low speed with hand mixer. Add egg to milk and whisk lightly, then add sherry. Pour into middle of dry ingredients. Stir until just blended, then fold in blueberries. Fill muffin cups ⅔ full. Bake 20 to 23 minutes at 400°.

Yield: 1 dozen muffins

CRANBERRY OAT BRAN MUFFINS

4 cups finely milled oat bran
1 cup quick-cooking rolled oats
1 cup chopped dried fruit
½ cup dried cranberries
2 tablespoons baking powder

2 medium eggs
1 cup firmly packed light brown sugar
1 (14-ounce) can sweetened condensed milk
1 (14-ounce) can water

Combine all ingredients together in a large mixing bowl. Stir until just moistened. Grease 2 muffin pans or line with paper muffin cups. Fill each muffin cup ⅔ full. Bake in a 425° oven for 17 minutes. Best when served warm.

Yield: 2 dozen muffins

APPLE CARROT MUFFINS

4 cups all-purpose flour
2½ cups sugar
4 teaspoons baking soda
4 teaspoons cinnamon
1 teaspoon salt
4 cups grated carrot
1 cup raisins
1 cup chopped pecans
1 cup sweetened shredded coconut
2 apples, peeled, cored and grated
6 large eggs
2 cups vegetable oil
4 teaspoons vanilla extract

Sift flour, sugar, baking soda, cinnamon and salt together in a large mixing bowl. Stir in grated carrots, raisins, pecans, coconut and apples. In a separate bowl, beat eggs with oil and vanilla extract and stir into the flour mixture until just blended. Spoon the batter into well-buttered ⅓ cup muffin tins, filling them to the top. Bake at 350° for 35 minutes or until top springs back when touched. Let cool in the tins on racks for 5 minutes before turning them out to cool completely.

Yield: 30 muffins

ZUCCHINI MUFFINS

½ cup sugar
1 large egg, lightly beaten
¼ cup vegetable oil
¾ cup all-purpose flour
¼ teaspoon baking powder
¼ teaspoon baking soda
¼ teaspoon salt
¼ teaspoon freshly grated nutmeg
1 cup grated zucchini (about ¼ pound)
¼ cup raisins, finely chopped
¼ cup chopped pecans

Preheat oven to 350°. Combine the sugar, egg and oil in a large bowl. Mix well. Sift the flour with the baking powder, baking soda, salt and nutmeg in a medium bowl. Stir this into the sugar-egg mixture. Add the zucchini, raisins and pecans and stir only until blended. Spoon the batter into a muffin tin, filling each cup about ⅔ full. Bake until the muffins are golden brown and a toothpick inserted in the center comes out clean, about 25 minutes. Run a knife around the edges to loosen.

Yield: 9 muffins

CARAMEL SWIRL COFFEE CAKE

½ cup chopped nuts	2 (8-ounce) packages
½ cup butter	refrigerator crescent
1 cup brown sugar	dinner rolls
	2 tablespoons water

Coat bottom and sides of a Bundt pan with cooking spray or butter. Sprinkle bottom of pan with 3 tablespoons nuts. Place remaining nuts, butter, brown sugar, and water in medium saucepan. Heat until just boiling, stirring frequently. Remove from heat. Unwrap rolls. Do not unroll. Cut into 8 wheel-type slices and arrange in a single layer in the Bundt pan, being careful to separate each wheel. Spoon ½ of sauce over arranged dough. Repeat for second can of rolls and pour remaining sauce over the dough. Bake 30 to 35 minutes at 350°. Cool for 3 minutes. Turn out onto plate and serve.

Yield: 8 to 12 servings

HIGH RISE APPLE PANCAKE

1 medium apple	½ cup plus 2 tablespoons all-purpose flour
1 teaspoon lemon juice	
2 tablespoons sugar	½ cup plus 2 tablespoons milk
1 teaspoon cinnamon	
3 eggs or one carton egg substitute	5 tablespoons butter
	powdered sugar

Preheat oven to 425°. Peel and slice apple into ¼-inch slices and place in a small mixing bowl. Toss with lemon juice, sugar and cinnamon. In large mixing bowl, combine flour and milk and mix until just incorporated. Add eggs and mix. Batter should be slightly lumpy. In skillet, heat butter until foamy. Remove from heat and quickly add batter. Arrange apples in a pinwheel design and place in oven. Bake for 25 minutes or until pancake is puffed up and golden brown. Sprinkle with powdered sugar and serve with warm apple sauce, syrup or jam.

Yield: 2 generous servings

ENGLISH MUFFIN LOAF

2	packages active dry yeast	¼	teaspoon soda
6	cups all-purpose flour	2	cups milk
1	tablespoon sugar	½	cup water
2	teaspoons salt	½	cup cornmeal

Combine yeast, 3 cups flour, sugar, salt and soda. Heat milk and water to almost boiling; add to dry ingredients and beat well. Stir in rest of flour to make a stiff dough. Butter 2 loaf pans and sprinkle with cornmeal. Spoon batter into pans. Sprinkle top with cornmeal. Let rise in warm place, about 45 minutes. Bake at 400° for 25 minutes. Remove from pans at once. Cool and slice. Delicious toasted.

Yield: 2 loaves

OATMEAL SCONES

½	pound butter	3⅓	cups all-purpose flour
½	pound sugar	1⅓	cups buttermilk
1⅓	cups uncooked oatmeal	1½	cups raisins
1	teaspoon salt		grated rind of 1 small
1	teaspoon baking soda		orange
1	teaspoon baking powder		

Cream together butter and sugar. Grind ½ of the oatmeal in a blender or food processor until well ground. Add the ground oatmeal, salt, baking powder, and baking soda to the butter and sugar. Then alternately add the non-ground oatmeal and flour with buttermilk. Add the raisins and orange rind. The dough will be soft and sticky. To roll out, generously flour dough, hands, rolling pin and surface; cut into ½-inch thick rounds; place on greased cookie sheet. If desired, wash rounds with an egg wash of 1 lightly beaten egg and 1 tablespoon of water. Bake for 15 to 20 minutes in a 375° oven. These freeze well. They may be split and toasted under a broiler.

Yield: 24 scones

BANANA NECTARINE BREAD

¼ cup butter
1 cup brown sugar
1 well-beaten egg
3 large very ripe bananas
2 peeled very ripe
   nectarines

1½ cups sifted all-purpose
    flour
1 teaspoon baking soda
½ teaspoon salt

In a large mixing bowl, cream together butter and sugar. In a separate bowl, mash bananas and nectarines. Add egg and mashed fruit to butter and sugar. Combine dry ingredients in a separate bowl and add to fruit mixture. Mix well. Pour into 9 x 5 x 3-inch loaf pan and bake for 1 hour in a 325° oven.

Yield: 1 loaf

BLUEBERRY ORANGE NUT BREAD

3 cups sifted all-purpose
   flour
¾ cup sugar
3 teaspoons baking powder
¼ teaspoon baking soda
1 teaspoon salt
3 eggs
½ cup milk

½ cup margarine, melted
1 tablespoon grated orange
   peel
⅔ cup orange juice
1 cup fresh, frozen or
   drained canned
   blueberries
½ cup chopped walnuts

Sift together in a large mixing bowl flour, sugar, baking powder, baking soda and salt. In a separate bowl, beat together eggs, milk, melted margarine, orange peel and orange juice. Stir into flour mixture until dry ingredients are just blended. Fold in blueberries and nuts. Pour into greased 9 x 5 x 3-inch loaf pan. Bake in a 350° oven for 60 to 70 minutes. Remove from pan and cool. Wrap in foil and store overnight in refrigerator before cutting to serve.

Yield: 1 loaf

MANDARIN ORANGE BREAD

1 egg
1 cup sugar
1 (5.5-ounce) can sliced
  mandarin oranges with
  juice, reserving several
  slices to garnish
1 cup all-purpose flour

1 cup chopped nuts
1 teaspoon baking soda
1 cup powdered sugar
3 ounces softened cream
  cheese
1 tablespoon butter

Combine egg, sugar, oranges and juice, flour, nuts, soda and salt in a large mixing bowl and beat with hand mixer. Bake in greased and floured 8 x 8-inch pan in a 350° oven for 30 minutes or until brown on top. Make icing by combining powdered sugar, cream cheese and butter in medium mixing bowl and beating with hand mixer until smooth. Spread on bread while it is still warm. Top with reserved mandarin orange sections for decoration.

Yield: 16 squares

PUMPKIN BREAD

1¾ cups all-purpose flour
1 teaspoon baking powder
1 teaspoon baking soda
¾ teaspoon salt
½ teaspoon cinnamon
½ teaspoon nutmeg
¾ cup brown sugar

¾ cup sugar
½ cup oil
2½ tablespoons water
2 eggs
1 teaspoon vanilla extract
1 cup pumpkin
½ cup chopped pecans

In a large mixing bowl, sift together flour, baking powder, baking soda and salt. Add to that cinnamon and nutmeg. Mix well. In a separate bowl beat until fluffy, sugars, oil and water. Add to dry ingredients and mix well. Add eggs and vanilla. Mix well again. Add pumpkin and nuts. Mix well. Pour into 2 greased loaf pans. Bake for 1 hour at 350°.

Yield: 2 loaves

BOURBON NUT BREAD

8 separated eggs
3 cups sugar
1 pound butter
3 cups sifted flour

½ cup bourbon
2 teaspoons vanilla extract
2 teaspoons almond extract
1 cup chopped pecans

Beat egg whites until soft peaks form. Gradually add 1 cup sugar and continue beating until stiff peaks form. Set aside. Cream butter with remaining sugar. Add egg yolks 1 at a time, beating well after each addition. Add flour 1 cup at a time, alternately with bourbon, mixing well. Stir in vanilla and almond extract and nuts. Gently fold in egg whites. Pour into 3 well-greased 9 x 5 x 3-inch loaf pans. Bake at 350° for 1 hour.

Yield: 3 loaves

RHUBARB BREAD

Bread:
2½ cups all-purpose flour
 ¾ teaspoon salt
 1 teaspoon baking soda
 ¾ cup butter
1½ cups brown sugar
 1 egg

2 teaspoons grated lemon peel
1 teaspoon lemon extract
1 cup buttermilk
2 cups diced rhubarb

Topping:
½ cup sugar

2 tablespoons softened butter

Preheat oven to 350°. In a large mixing bowl sift together flour, salt and soda. In a separate bowl, cream together butter and brown sugar until light and fluffy. Add egg and beat well. Stir in lemon peel and extract. Stir in flour alternately with buttermilk. Mix until just moistened. Fold in rhubarb. Pour into two 8 x 4 x 2½-inch loaf pans. Bake 55 to 60 minutes or until toothpick inserted in center comes out clean. Let stand for 10 minutes. Remove from pans. Make topping by combining sugar and softened butter until crumbly. Sprinkle over batter.

Yield: 2 loaves

POPPY SEED BREAD WITH ORANGE GLAZE

Bread:

½ cup margarine
½ cup vegetable oil
2 cups sugar
3 eggs
1½ cups milk
1½ teaspoons vanilla extract
1½ teaspoons almond extract
1½ teaspoons butter flavoring

3 cups all-purpose flour
1½ teaspoons baking powder
¼ teaspoon salt
2 to 3 tablespoons poppy seeds
2 tablespoons orange zest (optional)

Glaze:

¼ cup orange juice
½ teaspoon vanilla extract
½ teaspoon almond extract

½ teaspoon butter flavoring
⅔ cup sugar

Combine margarine, oil and sugar in a food processor; blend until smooth. Add eggs and blend. Add milk, vanilla and almond extract, butter flavoring and blend. Add flour, baking powder, salt and poppy seeds and blend. Add orange zest if desired. Pour batter into 2 greased 9 x 5 x 3-inch pans. Bake for 50 minutes at 325° or until a toothpick inserted in center comes out clean. Cool 10 minutes then remove from loaf pans. Combine glaze ingredients and mix until sugar is dissolved. Drizzle over tops of loaves. Let cool completely.

Yield: 2 loaves

STRAWBERRY WALNUT BREAD

1	pint, cleaned and hulled strawberries	½	teaspoon nutmeg
1	cup sugar	¼	teaspoon salt
2½	cups flour	3	eggs
1	teaspoon baking soda	⅓	cup vegetable oil
½	teaspoon cinnamon	1	teaspoon vanilla extract
		1	cup chopped walnuts

Preheat oven to 350°. Cut strawberries into ½-inch pieces and place in a medium-sized mixing bowl. Sprinkle with ½ cup sugar. Set aside. Combine flour, soda, cinnamon, nutmeg and salt in a separate bowl. Set aside. In a separate bowl, beat eggs and remaining ½ cup sugar. Add oil and vanilla. Add flour mixture and mix well. Add sugared strawberries and walnuts. Combine thoroughly. Pour into a greased 9 x 5 x 3-inch loaf pan. Bake for 45 minutes. Cool at least 15 minutes then remove from pan and continue to cool on a baking rack.

Yield: 1 loaf

BOSTON BROWN BREAD

2	cups all-bran	⅞	cup sugar
2	cups buttermilk	2	cups all-purpose flour
1	cup seedless raisins	2	teaspoons baking soda
2	tablespoons molasses	½	teaspoon salt

In large mixing bowl, combine all-bran, buttermilk and raisins. Let stand until well moistened. Add molasses and stir. In a separate bowl, sift together sugar, flour, baking soda and salt and stir into wet ingredients. Pour into 2 well-greased 9 x 5 x 3-inch loaf pans. Bake in a 350° oven for 1 hour. Good with butter or cream cheese.

Yield: 2 loaves

THREE FLOUR BRAIDED BREAD

2¼	cups white flour	1¼	cups whole wheat flour
2	tablespoons sugar	2	tablespoons molasses
1	tablespoon salt	1¼	cups rye flour
2	packages dry active yeast	2	tablespoons molasses
¼	cup softened margarine	1	teaspoon caraway seed
2¼	cups warm (120° to 130°) water	1	tablespoon cooking cocoa
1	cup white flour	1¼	cups white all-purpose flour
			milk

In a large mixing bowl, combine 2¼ cups white all-purpose flour, sugar, salt and yeast. Add margarine and warm water. Beat 2 minutes at medium speed using a hand mixer. Add 1 cup white all-purpose flour. Beat at high speed for 2 minutes. Divide batter into 3 bowls. Make whole wheat dough by adding 2 tablespoons molasses and 1¼ cups whole wheat flour into ⅓ of the batter. Knead until smooth and elastic, about 5 minutes. Make rye dough by adding 2 tablespoons molasses, caraway seed, cocoa and 1¼ cups rye flour into ⅓ of the batter. Knead until smooth and elastic, about 5 minutes. Make additional white dough by adding 1¼ cups white all-purpose flour to ⅓ of the dough. Knead until smooth and elastic, about 5 minutes. Cover each bowl and let rise in a warm place until doubled, about 1 hour. Punch dough down. On a floured board, divide 1 dough in half. Roll into a 15-inch rope. Repeat until there are 6 ropes; 2 for each separate dough. On a greased baking sheet, place 3 ropes, 1 of each dough. Braid ropes, pinching ends to seal. Repeat with remaining three ropes. Cover and let rise until doubled, about 1 hour. Brush with milk and bake in a 350° oven for 30 to 35 minutes. Cool on racks.

Yield: 2 loaves

HEAVENLY WHITE BREAD

2⅓ cups hot water (100°)
6 cups unbleached white flour
2 envelopes active dry yeast
⅓ cup honey

⅓ cup nonfat dry milk
⅓ cup virgin extra light olive oil
¼ cup coarse salt

In large mixing bowl, place hot water, honey, nonfat dry milk, active dry yeast and 2½ cups unbleached white flour. Beat by hand or with hand mixer for 10 minutes. Tightly cover with aluminum foil and let rise to bubbly "sponge" stage, approximately 45 minutes. Fold in virgin extra light olive oil, coarse salt, and 2½ cups unbleached white flour; knead for 10 minutes, adding additional flour as necessary. Press dough into large oiled bowl. Turn dough over, leaving oiled side up. Cover with a moist towel or aluminum foil. Allow to rise in a warm place until doubled in size, approximately 45 to 60 minutes. Punch down risen dough and knead into smooth ball. Allow to "rest" for 5 minutes. Shape into flat circular loaves. Place on an oiled cookie sheet and allow to rise for 15 to 20 minutes. Bake in a 350° oven for 20 to 30 minutes or until a light golden color. Allow to cool for 15 minutes. Freezes well.

Yield: 2 loaves

CHUCK WAGON CORN CAKES

½ cup all-purpose flour
2 teaspoons baking powder
½ teaspoon salt
1 cup cooked rice

1 cup whole kernel corn, cooked and drained
1 beaten egg
3 tablespoons milk

Sift dry ingredients together; stir in rice, corn and egg; mix well. Add milk to make a thin batter; stir well. Cook until golden brown on a hot griddle or in a well-oiled skillet, turning once to brown both sides.

Yield: 6 to 8 servings

JALAPEÑO CORN BREAD

1 cup all-purpose flour	1 medium onion, grated
4 teaspoons baking powder	3 tablespoons butter or
2 tablespoons sugar	margarine, melted
1 teaspoon salt	2 cups grated sharp
1½ cups cornmeal	Cheddar cheese
2 eggs	1 (7-ounce) can drained
1 cup buttermilk	chopped jalapeño peppers

Preheat oven to 400°. Sift flour, baking powder, sugar and salt together into large mixing bowl. Add cornmeal. Beat the eggs and stir them into the dry ingredients along with the buttermilk, grated onion, and 1 tablespoon of melted butter or margarine. Heat the remaining butter in a 9-inch cast iron skillet. Pour in ½ the batter smoothing it over the bottom of the pan with a knife. Sprinkle 1 cup of the cheese and the peppers on the batter. Add the remaining batter. Sprinkle the remaining cheese on top and place in oven for 30 minutes. Run a knife around edge of pan to loosen bread. Flip it over onto a plate. Place serving plate over bread and flip over again. Cheese side of bread is now up. Serve hot with plenty of butter.

Yield: 6 to 8 servings

CHEESE MUFFINS

2 sticks butter or margarine	2 tablespoons frozen or
8 ounces grated sharp	freeze-dried chives
Cheddar cheese	1 cup sour cream
	2 cups self-rising flour

Preheat oven to 375°. In saucepan, melt butter over medium heat. Remove from heat and add cheese. Stir well and let cool 2 minutes. Add chives and sour cream, stirring after each. Add flour and blend well. Fill ungreased muffin tins to top. Bake 10 to 12 minutes. Freezes well.

Yield: 3 to 4 dozen muffins

PROSCIUTTO BREAD

1 (¼ ounce) package dry active yeast
¼ cup warm water
pinch sugar
½ cup warm water
2 large eggs, lightly beaten
2 teaspoons fennel seeds
1 teaspoon salt

3 to 3½ cups all-purpose flour
1 cup minced onion
2 tablespoons olive oil
½ pound thinly sliced prosciutto, cut into thin strips
1 large egg yolk
1 teaspoon water

Preheat oven to 350°. In a small bowl, activate the yeast in ¼ cup warm water with the sugar for 15 minutes, or until it is foamy. Transfer the mixture to a large bowl and stir in ½ cup warm water, whole eggs, fennel seed, salt and enough of the flour to make a soft, but not sticky dough. Knead the dough on a floured surface for 8 to 10 minutes or until it is smooth and elastic. Form into a ball and place in a lightly oiled bowl, turn it to coat with the oil and let it rise covered with plastic wrap in a warm place for 1 to 1½ hours or until it has doubled in size. While dough is rising, in a skillet cook the onion in the olive oil over moderately low heat, stirring until it is softened. Punch down the dough and knead in the onions and prosciutto. Form dough into a round loaf tucking the seam side under. Put the loaf on a baking sheet seam side down and let rise covered loosely with a dampened dish towel for 30 minutes or until it has doubled in size. In a small bowl, whisk the egg yolk with 1 teaspoon water and brush the loaf evenly with the egg wash. Bake the bread in a preheated 350° oven for 30 to 40 minutes or until it sounds hollow when the bottom is tapped. Cool on a rack.

Yield: 1 loaf

CRANBERRY BREAD

2 cups all-purpose flour
1 cup sugar
2 teaspoons baking powder
½ teaspoon baking soda
2 teaspoons grated orange rind
½ cup orange juice
⅓ cup water (or orange juice)
1 well beaten egg (or 2 egg whites)
2 tablespoons salad oil
1 cup halved, raw cranberries
½ cup chopped nuts (optional)

Combine flour, sugar, baking powder and baking soda in a large mixing bowl. In a separate bowl, combine orange rind, orange juice, water, egg and oil. Add all at once to dried ingredients. Stir until just moistened. Stir in the halved cranberries and nuts if desired. Turn into a greased and floured 9 x 5 x 3-inch loaf pan. Bake at 350° for 60 minutes. Cool and refrigerate. Best if left a day or so before using.

Yield: 1 loaf

CARAWAY CHEESE PUFFS

1 package active dry yeast
1⅓ cups all-purpose flour
¼ teaspoon baking soda
1 cup cottage cheese
¼ cup water
2 tablespoons sugar
1 teaspoon salt
1 tablespoon butter
1 egg
2 teaspoons caraway seed
2 teaspoons grated onion
1 cup all-purpose flour

Put yeast, 1⅓ cups flour and baking soda in a large mixing bowl. In a saucepan or in the microwave, heat cottage cheese, water, sugar, salt and butter until butter melts. Add to dry ingredients. Add egg, caraway seed and onion. Beat together. Stir in 1 cup flour and set to rise for 1½ hours or until doubled in size. Divide into greased muffin tins. Cover with a cloth and let rise again for about 40 minutes. Bake at 400° for 12 to 15 minutes.

Yield: 1 dozen muffins

Pasta Cheese & Eggs

Steam engines were in short supply during the fire.

PASTA, CHEESE AND EGGS

ANGEL HAIR PASTA WITH FETA

½ pound angel hair pasta or
    capellini
3 tablespoons olive oil
1 medium tomato, diced

4 ounces crumbled Feta
    cheese
1 (3.2-ounce) can pitted
    ripe olives, drained and
    quartered

Prepare pasta according to package directions; drain. Add olive oil and tomatoes to pasta in a large saucepan. Cook over medium heat until hot, gently tossing. Add Feta cheese and olives.

Yield: 4 servings

ANGEL HAIR PASTA WITH LOBSTER SAUCE

2 tablespoons unsalted
    butter
1 tablespoon olive oil
½ cup chopped sun-dried
    tomatoes
4 to 5 green onions
6 to 8 fresh mushrooms
¾ cup sliced mixed red and
    green peppers
4 to 6 slices of bacon, fried
    and drained

1 to 2 cups chopped cooked
    lobster meat (may
    substitute shrimp)
1 (9-ounce) package angel
    hair pasta
2 cups heavy cream
    freshly ground pepper
1 tablespoon lemon juice
4 to 5 fresh basil leaves,
    chopped
    lemon, sliced to garnish
    fresh spinach (optional)

Sauté vegetables with olive oil and butter in pan until tender. Do not overcook. Crumble bacon. Add bacon and lobster to vegetables. Stir to coat and mix. Cook pasta according to package directions and drain. Combine drained pasta with vegetables, cream, lemon juice and pepper to taste. Heat until hot, do not boil. Garnish with lemon slices and fresh basil leaf. Serve on bed of fresh spinach, if desired.

Yield: 6 servings

FETTUCCINE WITH ARTICHOKES

½ cup unsalted butter
1 cup heavy cream
1 cup freshly grated
  Parmesan cheese
½ cup chopped pimiento

1 (9-ounce) package frozen
  artichoke hearts, thawed
  and halved
1 pound (plus 3-ounces)
  fresh fettuccine
  salt and pepper

Combine butter, cream, cheese, pimiento and artichokes in a skillet; heat thoroughly. Cook fettuccine according to package directions; drain. Pour sauce over hot pasta; toss lightly until pasta is coated. Add salt and pepper to taste. Serve immediately.

Yield: 6 servings

FETTUCCINE WITH SUN-DRIED TOMATOES AND WILD MUSHROOMS

¼ cup unsalted butter
¼ cup (about 3 medium)
  minced shallots
6 ounces fresh wild
  mushrooms, quartered
6 whole sun-dried
  tomatoes, sliced into
  ¼-inch strips

2 cups whipping cream
  salt and pepper
1 pound fettuccine
2 to 3 green onions, cut
  diagonally into ¼-inch
  strips

Melt butter in a large heavy skillet over medium heat. Add shallots and stir 1 minute. Add mushrooms and tomatoes and stir 3 minutes. Add cream; season generously with salt and pepper. Bring to a boil and reduce heat. Simmer until sauce is thick enough to coat the back of a spoon or reduces to ¼ quantity. Cook fettuccine until tender; drain well. Transfer to a large bowl; add sauce and toss. Garnish with green onions.

Yield: 6 servings

FETTUCCINE AND FRESH TOMATO VINAIGRETTE

1 (1-pound) package
  fettuccine or spaghetti
1 cup chopped peeled and
  seeded tomatoes
¼ cup chopped mixed fresh
  herbs

¼ cup fresh lemon juice
2 large chopped shallots or
  green onions
1 cup olive oil
  orange zest to garnish
  fresh sage to garnish

Cook pasta according to package directions. Mix pasta with remaining ingredients; stir well. Garnish each serving with a small mound of orange zest and a sprig of fresh sage. Serve at room temperature.

Yield: 4 servings

LINGUINE WITH BLUE CRAB SAUCE

2½ cups skinned and seeded
  ripe tomatoes, or 1 can
  Italian plum tomatoes,
  drained
⅓ cup olive oil
1 large green pepper, finely
  chopped
3 tablespoons finely
  chopped Italian parsley
2 large cloves garlic,
  minced

2 tablespoons tomato paste
1 tablespoon dried oregano
  dash dried hot pepper
  flakes
1 tablespoon fresh chopped
  basil or 1 teaspoon dried
6 cleaned blue crabs
  salt
1 pound linguine

Purée the tomatoes through a fine sieve; combine with olive oil, green pepper, parsley, garlic, tomato paste, oregano, hot pepper and basil in a large deep skillet; bring to a boil, add crabs; partially cover and cook 1 hour over low heat. Add salt to taste. In a separate big pot, cook pasta according to package directions; drain at once; pour immediately into a large heated bowl. Cover with sauce. Place crabs around the perimeter. Serve at once.

Yield: 6 servings

LINGUINE WITH WHITE CLAM SAUCE

⅓ cup vegetable oil
6 chopped green onions
   (about 1¼ cups)
2 large cloves garlic,
   minced
3 tablespoons all-purpose
   flour
1 handful chopped parsley
   (about ½ cup)
1 bay leaf
1 teaspoon chopped fresh
   lemon peel
½ teaspoon nutmeg
½ teaspoon basil

½ teaspoon oregano
   scant teaspoon salt
⅛ teaspoon pepper
2 (6½-ounce) cans minced
   clams
1 cup water
2 tablespoons fresh lemon
   juice
1 pound semolina linguine
   melted butter or
   margarine
   grated Romano or
   Parmesan cheese
   (optional)

Heat oil in heavy saucepan over medium-high heat. Sauté onions until soft, but not brown. Stir in garlic; sauté a minute. Stir in flour, ¼ cup parsley, bay leaf, lemon peel, nutmeg, basil, oregano, salt and pepper. Cook 1 or 2 minutes, stirring. Meanwhile, drain clams, reserving juice (about 1 cup). Heat juice and 1 cup water to nearly boiling. Stir into onion mixture. Add clams and lemon juice; simmer until bubbling gently, 5 to 10 minutes or until slightly thickened. Cook linguine according to package directions; drain and rinse well. Toss with small amount of melted butter and some grated cheese, if desired. Stir remaining parsley into bubbling clam sauce. Serve sauce over linguine.

Yield: 4 servings

SHRIMP AND FRESH HERB LINGUINE

12 ounces linguine or
fettuccine
2 tablespoons butter or
margarine
3 tablespoons olive oil
1½ pounds medium peeled
uncooked shrimp
8 cloves garlic, minced
⅓ cup chopped onion

⅔ cup bottled clam juice
½ cup dry white wine
¼ cup chopped fresh parsley
or 1 tablespoon dried
¼ cup chopped fresh dill or
1 tablespoon dried
salt and pepper to taste
1 tablespoon butter or
margarine

Cook linguine or fettuccine according to package directions; drain; add 1 tablespoon butter; toss; keep warm and set aside. In a large heavy skillet, heat olive oil over medium heat; add shrimp and sauté about 3 minutes or until just pink, stirring frequently; transfer to a large bowl. In skillet sauté garlic and onion in 1 tablespoon butter for approximately 2 minutes; add clam juice and wine. Increase heat and boil about 8 minutes until mixture is reduced by half; reduce heat to medium low; add shrimp to skillet; add parsley, dill, salt and pepper to taste. Boil about 3 minutes. Pour over warm pasta and toss to blend. Serve immediately.

Yield: 4 servings

PENNE WITH TUNA, CAPERS AND TOMATO SAUCE

olive oil
2 cloves garlic, minced
2 pounds fresh tuna
2 cups tomato sauce

½ cup white wine
2 tablespoons capers
1 pound penne pasta

In a large sauté pan, heat olive oil; sauté the garlic until golden brown; remove from the pan, and discard. Add the fresh tuna to the garlic oil; sauté until white in color. Remove the tuna from the pan. Add 2 cups of prepared tomato sauce and ½ cup white wine; simmer for 15 minutes. While the sauce is simmering, break up the cooked tuna into pieces; add to the sauce. Add the capers; simmer for 15 minutes. Taste for seasoning and caper flavor; add more capers if desired. Turn heat to low while pasta is cooking. Cook pasta according to package directions; drain; place on a warm serving platter. Pour tuna sauce over pasta. Serve immediately.

Yield: 6 servings

SPAGHETTI FLORENTINE

8 ounces spaghetti
2 (10-ounce) packages frozen chopped spinach
½ cup Parmesan cheese
4 tablespoons butter or margarine
2 slightly beaten eggs

½ cup chopped onion
3 cups sliced fresh mushrooms (about ¾ pound)
2 cups shredded mozzarella cheese
tomato sauce

Cook spaghetti according to package directions; drain. Cook spinach; drain. Combine spaghetti, spinach, Parmesan cheese, 2 tablespoons butter and eggs; mix well. Sauté onion and mushrooms in remaining butter; add to other mixture and mix with cheese. Turn into greased 1½ quart casserole dish. Cover and bake at 350° for 25 minutes (May be baked in 13 x 9 x 2-inch pan and cut into pieces). Serve with tomato sauce.

Yield: 8 servings

SPAGHETTI WITH MIXED SEAFOOD

½ cup olive oil
6 cloves garlic, finely chopped
16 shrimp, peeled and deveined
1 pound boneless cod
6 cups chopped and seeded Italian tomatoes
½ cup fish stock
½ cup chicken stock
½ cup dry white wine
fresh coarsely chopped basil leaves
½ teaspoon red pepper flakes
8 scrubbed and debearded mussels
8 washed littleneck clams
8 crab legs
6 tablespoons finely chopped parsley
1 pound spaghetti
grated Romano cheese

Heat olive oil in a heavy skillet. Add the garlic; sauté until translucent. Sauté shrimp in the pan over medium heat until pink. Add cod and sauté for 3 minutes; remove from pan and keep warm. Add tomatoes, stock, wine, basil and red pepper flakes to the pan and simmer for 20 minutes. Add mussels, clams, crab legs and parsley to the sauce; cook until seafood is done. In the meantime, cook the spaghetti according to package directions. Return the shrimp and cod to the sauté pan while pasta is cooking; simmer until the pasta is done. Drain pasta and place on a warm serving platter. Pour the sauce over the pasta and arrange seafood around the pasta. Garnish with parsley. Serve with Romano cheese.

Yield: 8 servings

PASTA WITH GREEN BEANS AND PINE NUTS

½ pound small bow or shell pasta
1 pound fresh green beans
1 cup halved cherry tomatoes
2 cups loosely packed fresh basil leaves
½ cup olive oil
4 cloves garlic
½ teaspoon salt, or to taste
½ cup freshly grated Parmesan cheese
¼ cup cubed Fontina cheese
3 tablespoons butter
2 tablespoons pine nuts
freshly ground black pepper

Cook pasta according to package directions; drain well; put into large bowl. Cook green beans in boiling water 4 to 6 minutes or until crisp-tender. Rinse under cold water to stop the cooking; drain well; add to pasta. Add cherry tomatoes and toss. Put basil leaves, oil, garlic and salt into food processor or blender; process until smooth. Add cheeses and butter; process until smooth. Add pine nuts and process until coarsely chopped. Add sauce and pepper to the pasta mixture; toss to coat. Serve at room temperature.

Yield: 4 to 6 servings

PASTA WITH WATERCRESS

1 pound cooked vermicelli
4 to 6 tablespoons olive oil
1 tablespoon sesame oil
1 large bunch minced watercress (coarse stems removed)
6 tablespoons toasted pine nuts
freshly ground pepper
salt to taste
few dashes hot pepper sauce

Add olive oil to pasta while the pasta is still warm and will readily absorb it. In wok or skillet, heat sesame oil and stir-fry watercress, 1 to 2 minutes or until wilted. Combine watercress and pine nuts, pepper and hot pepper sauce with pasta, mixing well so that all the strands absorb the herb and spices.

Yield: 4 servings

RISOTTO WITH LOBSTER AND SHRIMP

2	pounds medium shrimp	4	cups chicken broth
2	tablespoons olive oil	1	pound drained and
6	tablespoons sweet butter		crushed tomatoes
¼	pound boiled lobster meat		(canned or fresh)
½	cup dry white wine		salt and pepper to taste
2	cups Arborio rice		

Simmer shrimp in water until shrimp shell turns pink; remove the shrimp from water; peel and devein; set aside. For this dish you need two casseroles that can be used on a stove top. In the first casserole, melt 3 tablespoons butter over low heat; add 1 tablespoon olive oil. Add the shrimp and lobster; sauté for 3 minutes. Add wine and cook for 2 minutes longer; remove from heat; set aside. Melt the remaining butter in the second casserole; add 1 tablespoon olive oil. Add rice; sauté for 4 minutes or until all of the butter is incorporated. Add 1 cup of hot broth; stir well. Add the crushed tomatoes, mixing well, until all is incorporated. Simmer for about 18 minutes, stirring constantly. Slowly add additional broth until all is absorbed by the risotto, stirring constantly. When risotto is almost cooked, place the shrimp and lobster over low heat until risotto is done. Add wine to taste; stir well and add the shrimp and lobster. Serve immediately.

Yield: 6 servings

RISOTTO WITH FOUR CHEESES

4	ounces Gorgonzola cheese (crust removed)	2	cups Arborio rice
4	ounces mozzarella cheese	3½	cups chicken broth
4	ounces Italian Fontina cheese (crust removed)	½	cup white wine
1	cup lukewarm milk		salt and pepper to taste
4	ounces unsalted butter	6	tablespoons grated fresh Parmesan cheese
1	tablespoon olive oil		pine nuts
			fresh parsley

Cut the 3 cheeses into cubes of less than ½-inch. Put the cubes in a glass bowl with the warm milk and let stand until needed. Heat the butter and oil in a flame-proof casserole over medium heat. When the butter is melted, add the rice and sauté for 4 minutes. Heat the broth to a boil in a separate pan. Start adding broth to the rice, a small quantity at a time, stirring constantly until the rice has absorbed all the broth, for about 12 minutes. Add the wine and stir until well absorbed. Add the milk with all the cheeses to the pan and keep stirring until milk and cheeses are well mixed, about 6 minutes. Taste for salt and pepper. Add pine nuts and grated Parmesan cheese. Mix well and transfer to a serving dish. Top with fresh parsley.

Yield: 4 servings

CHICKEN AND LEMON RISOTTO

3 tablespoons lemon juice
2 large egg yolks
½ cup heavy cream
4 cooked chicken breasts (2 cups diced)
2 tablespoons butter
1 small peeled finely chopped onion

1½ cups Arborio rice
⅓ cup dry white wine
4 to 5 cups hot chicken stock
salt and freshly ground pepper to taste
3 tablespoons finely sliced fresh chives

In a bowl, combine the lemon juice, egg yolks and cream. Whisk with a fork until well blended and set aside. Dice the chicken and set aside. In a large heavy skillet, melt the butter. Add the onion and sauté until soft; add the rice and stir until coated; add the wine and cook over moderate heat until the wine disappears, stirring constantly. Start adding the broth ½ cup at a time, stirring constantly. Keep heat moderate so the liquid is absorbed, but not too quickly. Continue to add the stock ½ cup at a time, as the previous ½ cup is completely absorbed. After 20 minutes, start adding the stock ¼ cup at a time. Test to see if the risotto is still chewy or al dente. The entire process should take about 30 minutes. Before the risotto is done, approximately 5 minutes, stir in the lemon cream, add the chicken and the chives. Taste and correct the seasonings, adding the freshly ground pepper. Serve immediately.

Yield: 4 to 6 servings

SCALLOP RAVIOLI

Filling:

8 ounces scallops
5 tablespoons chilled whipping cream
¼ cup fresh bread crumbs
2½ tablespoons soft butter
2 egg yolks

1 tablespoon fresh chopped oregano or 1 teaspoon dried
1 teaspoon grated lemon zest
¼ teaspoon salt
⅛ teaspoon cayenne pepper

Ravioli:

1 (16-ounce) 20 wrapper package egg roll skins

Sauce:

½ cup unsalted butter
1 tablespoon fresh chopped oregano or 1½ teaspoons dried

salt and pepper to taste

To prepare the filling, combine 2 tablespoons cream and bread crumbs in small bowl. Purée scallops with bread crumb mixture in food processor container. Add 1½ tablespoons butter, egg yolks and oregano; process for 10 seconds. With machine running, add remaining 3 tablespoons cream. Transfer mixture to bowl. Add lemon zest, salt and cayenne. Cover and refrigerate for 30 minutes.

To make ravioli, cut each egg roll skin into 4 equal squares. Place 1 tablespoon of filling in the center of 2 of them and moisten the edges. Place remaining squares over them, pressing down around the filling to force air out and sealing the edges. Trim the excess dough around the filling with a fluted pizza cutter. Use remaining filling in the same way. Place the filled squares on a dry towel. Bring a pot of salted water to a boil and cook the ravioli in it, in batches, for about 2 minutes or until they rise to the surface. Drain on paper towels.

To make the sauce, melt butter in saucepan over low heat. Season with salt, pepper and oregano. Let sit as long as possible in a warm place such as over a pilot light flame for at least an hour. Serve hot over ravioli.

Yield: 2 servings

PORCINI MUSHROOMS WITH SPINACH PASTA

1   ounce Porcini
    mushrooms
1   cup water
2   tablespoons olive oil
4   tablespoons butter
½   onion, finely chopped
2   tablespoons ¼-inch wide
    prosciutto cubes

4   ripe medium tomatoes,
    peeled, seeded and
    chopped into ½-inch
    cubes, or 2 cups puréed
    canned Italian plum
    tomatoes
½   teaspoon salt
    freshly ground pepper
1   pound spinach pasta
1   to 2 cups freshly grated
    Parmesan cheese

Soak the mushrooms in a cup of warm water for 30 minutes; drain over cheesecloth; reserve the water. Rinse the mushrooms in cold water; drain well. Chop if the mushrooms are larger than ½-inch. Heat the oil and butter in a large skillet; when they reach bubble point, add the chopped onion; sauté for 3 minutes. Add the prosciutto and sauté another 2 minutes. Add tomatoes, salt, pepper, mushrooms, and mushroom liquid; cook, uncovered at a simmer for 40 minutes. Cook pasta according to package directions; drain well and return to the pot. Pour the sauce over the pasta. Serve with cheese to taste.

Yield: 6 servings

FUSILLI WITH PORCINI AND PROSCIUTTO

1 cup dried Porcini mushrooms	16 sun-dried tomatoes, each sliced into thin strips
olive oil	¼ cup chopped basil
3 cloves garlic, peeled	¼ cup heavy cream
¼ pound thinly sliced prosciutto, cut into short strips	white pepper
	½ cup imported Parmesan cheese
2 cups tomato sauce	¼ cup chopped Italian parsley
1 cup Italian red wine	½ pound Italian fusilli pasta

Soak mushrooms in cold water for 2 hours. In a large sauté pan, pour enough olive oil to coat the bottom of the pan. Sauté the garlic until golden in color; add the prosciutto, stirring constantly for 5 minutes; remove the prosciutto from the oil and garlic; place in a bowl; set aside. Add the mushrooms, (slice if too large), to the garlic and oil; sauté for 5 minutes. Add the tomato sauce, red wine and tomatoes; simmer for 15 minutes. While the sauce is simmering, cook the pasta according to package directions. Add chopped basil and cream to sauce; stir until all of the cream is incorporated into the sauce. Drain the pasta; add to the sauce; mix well. Place the pasta on a warm serving platter and top with grated Parmesan cheese and chopped parsley.

Yield: 4 servings

GRATIN OF PASTA AND SAUSAGE

1 pound Italian sausages, hot or mild	6 quarts water
1 cup heavy cream	salt and freshly ground pepper
4 tablespoons butter	¾ cup freshly grated imported Romano cheese
1 egg yolk, beaten	
1½ pounds dried fusilli pasta	

Prick the sausages on all sides with a fork and place in a skillet with just enough water to cover; bring to a boil, reduce heat to moderate and poach 5 minutes. Pour off water from the skillet and fry the sausages 15 to 20 minutes, turning occasionally; drain on paper towels and cut into thin rounds. Meanwhile, in a small saucepan, combine the cream, butter and egg yolk over moderate heat and simmer, stirring constantly with a whisk, about 1 minute or until mixture thickens; keep hot. Preheat oven to 325°. In a large pot, bring 6 quarts of salted water to a boil. Add the pasta, stir and cook al dente, drain; transfer to a large well-buttered gratin dish. Add the sausage and salt and pepper to taste; stir until well blended. Pour the cream mixture over the pasta and sausage, sprinkle the cheese on top and bake about 20 minutes or until the top is nicely browned.

Yield: 6 servings

BOWTIES WITH SPINACH AND RED ONIONS

1 pound fresh spinach	2 cups chicken broth
2 tablespoons butter	1 cup water
2 tablespoons olive oil	½ pound bowtie pasta
1 red onion, thinly sliced	½ cup grated cheese
1 clove garlic	freshly ground black
½ cup dry Italian white wine	pepper

Cook the spinach and drain well. Melt butter in a sauté pan. Add olive oil and red onion; sauté until soft. Add garlic and white wine; simmer for 10 minutes. Meanwhile, boil the broth and water in a pan large enough to cook the pasta. Cook the pasta al dente. Add the cooked spinach to the onion and garlic sauce; simmer until the pasta is done. Drain pasta; add to the sauce. If too dry, add some hot broth. Add grated cheese; serve hot with freshly ground black pepper.

Yield: 4 servings

CRUMB CRUST QUICHE

4 slices firm bread	2 cups filling of choice
5 tablespoons butter	½ cup cubed cheese
3 eggs	3 scallions, chopped
1 cup cream or half-and-half	1 tablespoon chopped chives
salt and pepper, to taste	

In a food processor or blender, make crumbs from the bread. In a large skillet, sauté the bread crumbs in butter until crumbs are golden and butter is absorbed. Pat the crumbs into a 9 or 10-inch pie pan, forming a pie crust shape. Over the crust, distribute any filling desired; broccoli flowerets, asparagus tips, peas, cooked shrimp, cubed ham, cooked chicken, etc. Lightly beat the eggs into the cream and pour over the filling. Sprinkle on cheese, onions and chives. Salt and pepper to taste. Bake at 350° for about 35 minutes or until tart is set. Crumbs will have solidified and formed a crust which can be cut into slices like a pie. Serve hot or at room temperature.

Yield: 6 to 8 servings

BELGIAN EGGS WITH HAM

16	slices firm textured bread	½	teaspoon nutmeg
8	ham slices (about ½ pound), cut ½-inch thick	½	teaspoon salt
4	eggs, separated	½	teaspoon pepper
1½	cups (about 6 ounces) grated Gruyère cheese		vegetable oil for frying
		½	teaspoon paprika

Preheat oven to 350°. With a 2½-inch round cutter or glass, cut the bread and ham into 16 rounds each. In a small bowl, mix the egg yolks and cheese until blended to a paste. Stir in nutmeg, salt and pepper. Place a round of ham on each round of bread. Spread 1 tablespoon of cheese mixture evenly over each round. Pour enough oil into a medium skillet to measure ¼-inch deep. Warm over moderate heat until hot, but not smoking. Meanwhile, beat the egg whites until stiff, but not dry. Spoon 1 heaping tablespoon of the beaten egg whites onto each round to form a cone-shaped top. Smooth out the edges to completely cover the rounds to the rim. Fry in hot oil, 3 or 4 at a time, for about 1 minute until the bread is golden brown. With a slotted spatula immediately transfer rounds to a baking sheet. When all the rounds are fried, bake them for about 8 minutes until the egg whites are golden. Serve hot.

Yield: 8 servings

CRUNCHY STUFFED EGGS

4	hard boiled eggs		salt and pepper to taste
2	ounces grated sharp Cheddar or Swiss cheese	1	tablespoon half-and-half
1	ounce chopped walnuts	1	small head lettuce
		2	sliced tomatoes

Cut eggs in half lengthwise and remove yolks. Place the yolks in a bowl and add cheese, nuts, half-and-half, salt and pepper. Mix well. Pile mixture back into egg whites. Serve on a bed of lettuce and garnish with slices of tomato.

Yield: 4 servings

CREOLE EGGS

Eggs:

2	cups (12-ounces) grated Cheddar cheese	2	teaspoons Dijon mustard
½	cup butter	1	cup half-and-half (or 1 cup milk and ½ stick melted butter)
½	teaspoon salt		
¼	teaspoon pepper	12	eggs, lightly beaten

Creole Sauce:

1	cup chopped onions	1	tablespoon tomato paste
2	celery ribs, cut up	1	teaspoon chili powder
1	small green pepper, cut up	1	teaspoon brown sugar
2	cloves garlic	1	bay leaf
1	tablespoon oil	¼	teaspoon dried thyme
2	tablespoons butter	2	cups beef bouillon
2	(8-ounce) cans tomatoes, drained and broken into small pieces		hot pepper sauce to taste

Butter a 13 x 9 x 2-inch casserole dish. Spread grated cheese evenly over the bottom. Dot with stick of butter. Combine salt, pepper, mustard and cream. Pour ½ of mixture gently over cheese. Beat 12 eggs with whisk until yolks are blended with whites, but not frothy. Pour over cheese layer. Drizzle remaining cream mixture over top. Bake at 325° for 30 to 40 minutes. Allow to sit before serving so butter is absorbed.

To make sauce, chop onion, celery, green pepper and garlic cloves by hand or in food processor. Sauté in oil and butter. Add tomatoes, and remaining ingredients (except for hot pepper sauce); simmer for 1 hour, stirring from time to time. Add hot pepper sauce to taste at end of cooking. Cut egg casserole into 10 pieces. Serve Creole Sauce over the top of each slice. (Makes about 3½ cups).

Yield: 10 to 12 servings

FLORENTINE EGGS WITH ARTICHOKES

4 frozen artichoke hearts
2 teaspoons fresh lemon
   juice
1 tablespoon butter
2 tablespoons olive oil
¼ cup all-purpose flour

4 eggs
2 tablespoons water
   salt and pepper
   ripe black olives to
   garnish

Slice thinly and vertically the artichoke hearts and allow them to thaw. Pat the sliced artichokes in paper towels; sprinkle them with lemon juice. In an oven-proof skillet, melt the butter and add oil until hot. Dredge the artichokes in flour and cook them slowly in the hot skillet mixture until golden brown. In a bowl, beat the eggs, water, salt and pepper just until blended. Pour over the artichokes and bake at 350° for about 10 minutes or until the eggs are set. Serve from the skillet. Garnish with ripe black olives.

Yield: 4 servings

EGGS MEXICANO

8 eggs
½ cup whipping cream
   salt and pepper to taste
1 ripe avocado
   lemon juice

1 tablespoon butter
1 cup cubed Jarlsberg
   cheese
1 cup seasoned croutons
   Mexican salsa to taste

In a medium bowl, beat eggs lightly; add cream, salt, and pepper. Dice avocado; sprinkle with lemon juice; set aside. Melt butter in large skillet; add egg mixture. Stir over medium heat until mixture begins to set. Add cheese and gently stir until melted. Fold in croutons and avocado; remove from heat. Spoon on Mexican salsa and serve immediately.

Yield: 4 servings

EGGS AU GRATIN

1 pound cleaned trimmed quartered fresh mushrooms
2 sticks butter
2 tablespoons minced shallots or green onions
salt and pepper to taste
6 tablespoons all-purpose flour

2 cups hot milk
1 cup whipping cream
fresh lemon juice
12 to 16 eggs
½ cup grated Parmesan cheese, or a mixture of Parmesan, Cheddar and/or Swiss

Sauté mushrooms in 3 tablespoons butter in a large skillet over high heat 5 to 6 minutes or until they begin to brown. Stir in the shallots; cook and toss over medium heat 1 to 2 minutes. Season to taste with salt and pepper; reserve. Melt 5 tablespoons of butter in a heavy bottomed saucepan. Stir in flour; cook and stir over low heat 2 minutes without coloring. Remove from heat; whisk in hot milk. Beat in half of the cream; add salt and pepper to taste; simmer, stirring 4 to 5 minutes until thickened. Whisk in remaining cream (excluding 1 tablespoon), a few teaspoons at a time until sauce coats a spoon, but is not too thick. Taste and adjust seasonings, adding lemon juice to taste. Pour remaining tablespoon of cream on top of sauce to prevent a skin from forming. Beat the eggs, salt and pepper in a medium bowl until blended. Melt 3 tablespoons butter in a large skillet; pour in the eggs and stir over moderately low heat. When the eggs slowly begin to thicken in 2 to 3 minutes, stir rapidly until they scramble into very soft curds. Eggs should be slightly underdone; they will finish cooking under the broiler. Immediately remove the eggs from the heat and stir in 1 or 2 additional table-spoons of butter. Spoon a thin layer of the sauce into the bottom of a 12 x 9 x 2-inch oval baking dish. Sprinkle with 2 tablespoons of the cheese. Spoon in half of the eggs. Fold in a cup of the sauce into the mushrooms and spoon over the eggs. Sprinkle with 3 more table-spoons of cheese. Top with remaining eggs; pour over remaining sauce; sprinkle with remaining cheese; dot with remaining butter. At serving time, broil mixture 4 inches from heat source for 1 to 2 minutes or until golden. Serve immediately.

Yield: 6 to 8 servings

EGGS WITH PROVOLONE CHEESE

12 pitted black olives
3 tablespoons olive oil
2 ounces diced Provolone
   cheese

4 eggs, well beaten
  salt and pepper
1 tablespoon finely chopped
  sage or 1 teaspoon dried

Cut olives in half. Heat oil in skillet; add olives and sauté for 2 minutes. Add cheese; stir for 1 minute over medium heat. Fold in eggs. Add salt, pepper and sage to taste. Stir until eggs are cooked, but not dry. Serve hot.

Yield: 2 to 3 servings

RAMEKIN BAKED EGGS

3 eggs
  a little milk
½ tablespoon dry mustard
  salt and pepper to taste
1 tablespoon chopped black
  olives
1 tablespoon green peppers

1 tablespoon green onion
1 tablespoon mushrooms
¼ cup grated Cheddar
  cheese (sharp or other)
  non-stick vegetable spray
  paprika

Heat oven to 350°. Mix together 2 eggs, milk, mustard, salt and pepper, whisk as you would scrambled eggs; set aside. Grease an individual ramekin with a non-stick vegetable spray. Add the chopped vegetables and grated cheese. Pour scrambled egg mixture over the ingredients. Break one whole egg on top of ramekin. Add a dash of paprika. Bake until egg sets. This can be frozen before the whole egg is added.

Yield: 1 serving

OVEN SCRAMBLED EGGS

12 eggs
1 (8-ounce) package cream
   cheese, cubed
1 teaspoon salt

1 teaspoon pepper
2½ cups hot milk
½ cup butter or margarine,
   melted

Mix all ingredients together and beat lightly. Pour into casserole dish. Bake at 350° for 45 minutes.

Yield: 10 servings

PASTA FRITTATA WITH CHEESE AND JALAPEÑO PEPPERS

2 jalapeño peppers, seeded
6 large green onions, cut in
   1-inch pieces
1 cup fresh cilantro
6 ounces colby cheese
6 ounces Monterey Jack
   cheese

1 large egg
¾ teaspoon salt, or to taste
1 medium red pepper
3 cups cooked linguine
2 tablespoons peanut oil
   salsa and sour cream

Mince the peppers, green onions, cilantro and both cheeses in a food processor. Add the egg and salt; mix well. Transfer to a large bowl. Cut the red pepper into 2-inch by ⅛-inch strips. Add them to the bowl with the linguine and mix gently, but thoroughly. Heat a 12-inch ovenproof skillet over medium heat. When it is hot, add the oil and brush it over the entire surface, including the sides. When it is sizzling hot, add the pasta mixture, quickly spreading it in an even layer over the entire bottom. Cook until browned on the bottom, about 6 minutes. Transfer it to a preheated broiler and broil 6-inches from the heat for 2 to 3 minutes. Serve with salsa and sour cream as toppings.

Yield: 6 servings

ZUCCHINI AND PROSCIUTTO FRITTATA

2	tablespoons melted butter	½	cup fine bread crumbs
¼	cup chopped prosciutto	¼	cup grated Parmesan
1½	cups chopped cooked		cheese
	drained zucchini	¼	teaspoon salt
4	eggs, lightly beaten	¼	teaspoon onion salt
½	cup milk	¼	teaspoon pepper

Melt butter and sauté prosciutto for 2 minutes. Combine all ingredients. Turn into shallow buttered round casserole dish. Bake at 375° for 25 to 30 minutes or until set. Cut into wedges. Serve as vegetable or main dish.

Yield: 4 servings

RATATOUILLE WITH EGGS

⅓	cup olive oil	2	cups cubed red ripe
1	pound peeled eggplant,		tomatoes
	cut into 1-inch cubes	3	tablespoons tomato paste
1	pound unpeeled zucchini,	1	bay leaf
	cut into 1-inch cubes	½	teaspoon dried thyme
1	cup cubed seeded green		salt and pepper to taste
	pepper	8	eggs
1	cup cubed onion	¼	cup freshly grated
1	tablespoon minced garlic		Parmesan cheese

Heat oil in a heavy frying pan until very hot. Add eggplant and zucchini; cook, stirring often, for about 2 minutes. Add green pepper and onion; cook about 6 minutes, stirring. Add garlic; stir again. Add tomatoes, tomato paste, bay leaf and thyme. Add salt and pepper to taste. Heat to boil, stirring. Spoon into a 13 x 9 x 2-inch ovenproof baking dish; place casserole in a 400° oven for 20 minutes. Remove from oven and make 8 indentations in the center of ratatouille; break 1 egg into each indentation. Sprinkle cheese evenly over the surface of the dish. Return to oven and bake 30 minutes more.

Yield: 4 servings

CHEESY GRITS

1 cup grits	2 eggs
2 cups boiling water	1¼ cups grated sharp
1 teaspoon salt	Cheddar cheese
1 cup milk	1 clove garlic, minced
1 stick butter	paprika
¾ teaspoon red pepper	

In a heavy saucepan, cook grits in boiling water and salt until thickened. Add milk and lower heat. Cover and continue cooking over low heat. Add butter and red pepper. Beat eggs and stir into mixture. Add 1 cup grated cheese and garlic. Turn into buttered casserole dish. Sprinkle with remaining ¼ cup grated cheese and paprika for color. Bake in a 350° oven for 45 minutes or until it rises and turns a golden brown.

Yield: 8 servings

FRENCH TOAST CASSEROLE

1 long loaf French bread, about ½ pound	¾ teaspoon salt
	1 tablespoon vanilla extract
8 large eggs	2 tablespoons butter, cut
3 cups milk	into small pieces
4 teaspoons sugar	syrup or honey

Generously butter a 13 x 9 x 2-inch baking dish. Cut bread into 1-inch thick slices and arrange bread slices in single layer over bottom of prepared dish. Beat eggs, milk, sugar, salt and vanilla in large bowl until mixed. Pour over bread; cover with foil. Refrigerate overnight. Heat oven to 350°. Remove casserole from refrigerator and uncover; it is not necessary to bring casserole to room temperature. Dot top with butter pieces. Bake, uncovered, for 45 to 50 minutes, or until bread is puffy and lightly browned. Serve with your favorite syrup or honey.

Yield: 6 to 8 servings

ENTREES

Chicago's weary firemen struggled to control the flames.

ENTREES

CHICKEN BREASTS WITH BRIE, ALMONDS, CHUTNEY AND RED PEPPER

4 large boneless skinless
chicken breasts, halved
½ teaspoon lemon juice
½ cup strong chicken stock
½ cup white vermouth
1 teaspoon salt or less if
stock has salt
4 large Romaine leaves,
washed, dried and tough
white end trimmed

4 tablespoons tarragon-
flavored mayonnaise
8 ounces ripe Brie cheese
4 tablespoons sliced
almonds
4 tablespoons melted butter
1 roasted red pepper,
skinned, seeded and
chopped
½ cup good chutney to
garnish

In a large skillet, combine the lemon juice, chicken stock, vermouth and salt. Bring to a simmer, add chicken and poach until cooked, but still tender. The chicken will just be springy to the touch when done. Remove chicken and reserve. Chicken may be prepared the day before, stored in refrigerator and briefly warmed in the reserved stock, being careful not to overcook. Place a Romaine leaf on each of four plates. Spread 1 tablespoon of mayonnaise around the center of each leaf. Set aside plates. Place the chicken breasts on a broiler pan, divide the Brie into 4 slices and arrange them on the chicken breasts. Sprinkle on the almonds and drizzle with the melted butter. Broil 6 inches from flame, broiling slowly until cheese begins to run and almonds are lightly browned. Place one breast on each Romaine leaf, garnish with a little chutney and a red pepper mound to the side. Serve warm or at room temperature.

Yield: 4 servings

CHICKEN BREASTS WITH ROSEMARY AND LEMON

2 whole skinless boneless chicken breasts
¼ cup all-purpose flour
 salt and pepper to taste
1 tablespoon vegetable oil
1 tablespoon butter
2 tablespoons fresh rosemary or 1 tablespoon dried
4 cloves garlic, unpeeled
½ cup white wine
2 tablespoons fresh lemon juice
 chopped parsley

Thoroughly dredge chicken in flour seasoned with salt and pepper. Heat oil and butter in skillet. Add chicken pieces, rosemary and garlic. Cook about 4 minutes until pieces are brown on one side. Turn and cook, uncovered, 4 to 5 minutes until golden brown on the other side. Pour off all the fat from the skillet, leaving the chicken, rosemary and garlic in the skillet. Pour in wine and bring to a boil; add lemon juice and parsley. Cover tightly and cook 3 minutes longer. Remove and discard garlic; serve immediately.

Yield: 4 servings

CHICKEN WITH ORANGE SAUCE

8 boneless chicken breasts
½ cup all-purpose flour
½ teaspoon salt
1 teaspoon garlic salt
½ teaspoon paprika
5 tablespoons butter
⅓ cup almonds
1 to 2 tablespoons cornstarch
1 (6-ounce) can frozen orange juice
½ cup water
1 teaspoon rosemary
¼ teaspoon thyme

In a large bowl, mix flour, salt, garlic salt and paprika. Dredge the chicken in flour mixture. Sauté almonds in butter until golden and set aside. Brown chicken in drippings. In a separate pan, heat to a boil cornstarch, orange juice, water, rosemary and thyme. Place chicken in a single layer into a 13 x 9 x 2-inch baking dish. Pour cooked orange juice mixture over chicken. Bake in a 350° oven for 1 hour. Before serving, sprinkle with almonds.

Yield: 4 servings

STILTON CHICKEN

6 chicken breast halves, boned and skinned
all-purpose flour
6 tablespoons unsalted butter
salt and pepper
¾ cup unsalted chicken stock
¾ cup port
1½ cups heavy cream
3 pears, peeled, cored and cut into sixths
2 to 3 tablespoons Stilton cheese
2 tablespoons minced fresh parsley

Flatten the chicken breasts slightly. Sprinkle lightly with flour. In a heavy skillet, heat 4 tablespoons butter over medium flame; add the chicken. After 4 minutes, turn the chicken and sauté until springy to the touch. Remove to a warm platter. Sprinkle the breasts with salt and pepper, tent with foil and set in a 200° oven. Add stock and port to the same skillet and boil, reducing by half. Add the cream and boil until it is reduced to a sauce-like consistency. Meanwhile, in a small skillet, sauté the pear slices for 5 minutes in the remaining 2 tablespoons of butter. Set aside. Add 2 tablespoons of the Stilton to the port sauce and stir until melted. Taste the sauce and add additional Stilton if desired. Place the chicken on plates and top each with 3 pear slices, some of the sauce and minced parsley.

Yield: 6 servings

CHICKEN WITH LIME BUTTER

6 chicken breasts, skinned, boned, and halved
½ teaspoon salt
½ teaspoon pepper
⅓ cup vegetable oil

1 lime, juiced
8 tablespoons butter
½ teaspoon minced chives
½ teaspoon dill

Sprinkle chicken breasts on both sides with salt and pepper. Into a large skillet, pour vegetable oil and heat to medium temperature. Cook chicken 4 minutes or until lightly browned; turn chicken once; cover and reduce heat to low and continue cooking 10 minutes more or until fork can be inserted into chicken with ease. Remove chicken and keep warm; drain oil and discard. In same pan, cook lime juice over low heat until juice begins to bubble; add butter, stirring until butter becomes opaque and forms a thickened sauce; stir in chives and dill. Spoon sauce over chicken. Serve immediately.

Yield: 6 servings

STUFFED CHICKEN BREASTS

4 whole chicken breasts, boned (leave the two halves connected), with skin left on
¾ pound ricotta or drained cottage cheese
½ pound finely chopped Swiss chard or spinach leaves

2 finely chopped broccoli flowerets
salt and pepper to taste
½ teaspoon thyme
½ teaspoon tarragon
¼ teaspoon freshly grated nutmeg
4 tablespoons butter

In a bowl, mix together the cheese, Swiss chard, broccoli, thyme, tarragon and nutmeg. Using a sharp knife slit the connecting tissue of the chicken on one side and with your fingers lift the connecting tissue to form a pocket, leaving the sides still attached. Stuff each breast with enough of the mixture to form a compact pouch. Fold the sides of the breast underneath. Place breasts in a shallow roasting pan. Top each with a tablespoon of butter and bake at 350° for about 1 hour or until top is golden and stuffing starts to ooze out. Do not separate the breast halves. Cut into 1-inch slices by cutting across both breasts. Can be served hot or cold.

Yield: 6 to 8 servings

CHICKEN PARMESAN

1 (3-pound) chicken, cut up and skinned
⅓ cup sliced green onions
½ teaspoon thyme
1 tablespoon Dijon mustard
½ teaspoon cayenne pepper
3 tablespoons lemon juice

½ cup plain yogurt
½ cup mayonnaise
1 teaspoon salt
½ teaspoon pepper
½ cup grated Parmesan cheese

Place chicken pieces in a large shallow baking dish. Mix onions, thyme, mustard, cayenne pepper, lemon juice, yogurt and mayonnaise; spread mixture on chicken; sprinkle with salt, pepper and Parmesan cheese. Bake, uncovered, for 45 minutes at 350°. This dish freezes well.

Yield: 4 servings

ROASTED CHICKEN WITH LEMON CREAM SAUCE

Roasted Chicken:

1 large roasting chicken (not a broiler), 5 to 8 pounds

handful fresh herbs - stems included (tarragon, sage, marjoram, thyme, oregano, basil)
salt and pepper to taste

Lemon Cream Sauce:

½ cup butter
2 tablespoons sherry
2 tablespoons white wine
  juice and rind of 1 lemon
  rind of 1 orange

2 teaspoons lemon juice
  salt and pepper to taste
1 cup cream
½ cup imported Parmesan cheese

Stuff the cavity of a large roasting chicken with rinsed fresh herbs; salt and pepper. Roast at 325° to 350° until done, allowing about 2½ hours. Chicken is done when leg moves freely and juices just run clear; do not overcook. Allow 20 minutes for cooked chicken to rest before cutting into serving pieces.

To make the sauce, melt butter in a large skillet; stir in sherry and wine; add the grated rind of the lemon and the orange, the lemon juice and the salt and pepper. Turn up heat and stir the cream in slowly. Put in the chicken pieces and heat for a few minutes. Arrange chicken on a large serving dish that can go under the broiler. Pour sauce over the chicken and sprinkle with Parmesan cheese. Brown under the broiler and serve. Do not refrigerate the cooked roasting chicken before serving. The sauce may be made the day before.

Yield: 6 to 8 servings

GIDLEIGH PARK CHICKEN

Chicken:
4 pieces of chicken	sherry wine vinegar
salt and pepper to taste	3 cloves garlic, unpeeled

Sauce:
1 cup chicken stock	salt and pepper to taste
1 cup heavy cream	

Salt and pepper chicken and sauté in a little oil in a heavy frying pan with lid. When chicken is brown, pour out excess oil, leaving chicken in pan. Sprinkle 1 tablespoon sherry wine vinegar over chicken. Add garlic. Cover pan, lower heat and cook 15 to 20 minutes until chicken is done. Continue sprinkling chicken with more vinegar every 5 minutes while chicken is cooking. When done, remove the chicken from the pan and keep warm while making the sauce. To prepare sauce, deglaze the skillet with 1 cup chicken stock; reduce stock to about one half. Add 1 cup heavy cream and cook until slightly thickened. Add more vinegar to taste, salt and pepper if needed.

Yield: 4 servings

CHICKEN MARSALA

4 chicken breasts, skinned, split and boned	1½ cups dry Marsala wine
6 egg yolks	1 tablespoon lemon juice
1 cup Parmesan cheese	1 pound sliced fresh mushrooms
⅔ cup butter	3 tablespoons basil
⅔ cup olive oil	2 tablespoons parsley
1½ cups sweet Marsala wine	1 loaf toasted French bread

Pound chicken breasts until very thin. Dip in egg yolk, then in Parmesan cheese. Keep refrigerated for 3 hours. In large skillet, pour butter and olive oil. Over low heat sauté chicken until golden brown on both sides. Add sweet and dry Marsala, lemon juice, mushrooms, basil and parsley. Heat through another 8 to 10 minutes. Serve on toasted French bread.

Yield: 6 to 8 servings

SPANISH CHICKEN

12 skinless chicken breasts and thighs
2 cups pitted prunes or dried apricots or dried pears
1¼ cups white wine
¾ cup dark brown sugar
¾ cup olive oil
¾ cup red wine vinegar
¾ cup pitted green olives
¾ cup capers
4 tablespoons dried oregano
½ teaspoon crushed red pepper
6 medium bay leaves
1 small clove garlic, minced
3 tablespoons chopped cilantro
salt and pepper to taste

In 2 large baking pans, arrange chicken pieces in one layer. Combine all ingredients except cilantro and ½ cup brown sugar in large mixing bowl. Pour mixture over chicken so that prunes, olives and capers are evenly distributed. Cover and refrigerate overnight. Preheat oven to 350°. Sprinkle remaining brown sugar over the chicken and bake for about 1 hour, basting frequently. To serve, arrange chicken pieces with the sauce on a platter. Sprinkle with the cilantro.

Yield: 12 to 14 servings

SOUTHWESTERN GRILLED CHICKEN

4 to 6 boneless chicken breasts
¼ cup salsa
2 tablespoons fresh lime juice
1 tablespoon vegetable oil
1 clove garlic, minced
¼ teaspoon chili powder

Combine all ingredients except chicken in a bowl and stir well to make marinade. Marinate chicken in mixture for several hours. Cook chicken on preheated hot grill about 20 minutes, turning half way through cooking time.

Yield: 4 to 6 servings

CHICKEN WITH RUM SAUCE

2 frying chickens,
  quartered
½ teaspoon pepper
1 teaspoon ginger
1 teaspoon seasoned salt
1 teaspoon sugar
¼ cup soy sauce
1 cup rum
  juice of 1 lemon

1 cup orange juice
1 cup dry vermouth
  dash hot pepper sauce
1 red onion, sliced into
  rings
1 tablespoon grated orange
  peel
1 tablespoon grated lemon
  peel

Sprinkle chicken with pepper, ginger, seasoned salt and sugar. Brown chicken on both sides; add soy sauce, rum, lemon juice, orange juice, vermouth and dash of hot sauce to drippings; simmer 5 minutes. Place chicken in 13 x 9 x 2-inch baking pan; pour sauce over chicken. Bake at 325° for 45 minutes. Baste several times. Top with onion rings, sliced thin, and bake for another 15 minutes. Pour liquid into saucepan, add orange and lemon peel and simmer until thick. Spoon chicken onto platter; pour sauce over chicken. This dish can be frozen or prepared the day ahead.

Yield: 6 to 8 servings

THAI CHICKEN

1½ pounds skinless, boneless
  chicken fillets
  butter or margarine
⅔ cup creamy peanut butter
1 cup soy sauce
½ cup lemon juice
¼ cup brown sugar

4 cloves garlic, crushed
¼ teaspoon hot sauce (or
  more to taste)
½ cup medium sherry
1 cup water
  chopped scallions to
  garnish

Sauté chicken in butter or margarine or grill on gas grill. Combine all other ingredients except water in heavy saucepan. Stir sauce over moderate heat until boiling and smooth. Add water as necessary. The sauce should be thick and smooth. Remove sauce from heat and keep warm. Assemble cooked chicken on platter with sauce spooned on top.

Yield: 4 servings

ORIENTAL GRILLED CHICKEN

4 to 6 boneless breasts of chicken
½ cup fresh lemon juice
4 tablespoons chopped green onions
2 tablespoons soy sauce
2 tablespoons vegetable oil
1 teaspoon grated fresh ginger
¼ teaspoon red pepper flakes

Combine all ingredients except chicken in bowl and stir well to make marinade. Marinate chicken in mixture several hours. Cook chicken on preheated hot grill, about 10 minutes, turning half way through cooking time.

Yield: 4 to 6 servings

STIR-FRY CHICKEN AND PEA PODS

Sauce:
½ cup chicken broth
2 tablespoons soy sauce
1 tablespoon cornstarch
1 tablespoon sugar

Chicken:
1 pound chicken breasts, sliced in thin strips (may substitute deveined shrimp or thinly sliced beef, if so, add ¼ teaspoon red pepper flakes)
1½ tablespoons cornstarch
1 tablespoon soy sauce
1 tablespoon dry sherry
5 tablespoons vegetable oil
1 teaspoon minced garlic
⅓ cup sliced onions
⅓ cup celery
⅓ cup sliced mushrooms
⅓ cup bean sprouts
1 (6-ounce) thawed package frozen pea pods, or fresh

In small bowl, mix all sauce ingredients; set aside. In medium bowl, combine chicken, cornstarch, soy sauce and sherry; mix well and set aside. Marinate chicken for 15 minutes. In wok or large skillet, heat 3 tablespoons oil; add garlic and chicken; cook until no longer pink. Remove. Add 2 tablespoons oil, onion and celery. Cook 1 minute. Add mushrooms, sprouts, pea pods and sauce and cook stirring constantly until hot. Pour over chicken and serve on a bed of rice.

Yield: 2 to 4 servings

HUNAN CHICKEN AND VEGETABLES

4 chicken breasts, boned
  and sliced into 1 x ½-inch
  strips
  bottled Hunan sauce
2 small red bell peppers
3 scallions, sliced into
  ½-inch sections
2 small carrots
2 small yellow squash

2 celery stalks
4 cauliflower flowerets
2 large cloves garlic
1 good sized chunk of fresh
  ginger
2 cups sliced mushrooms
¼ cup sesame oil
¾ cup bean sprouts

Marinate chicken in Hunan sauce for at least 45 minutes. Slice very thin red pepper, scallions, carrots, squash, celery and cauliflower. Finely mince garlic and ginger. Heat oil in wok or large skillet. Sauté chicken about 2 minutes on each side. Add all vegetables except bean sprouts and stir for about 2 to 3 minutes. During the last minute, add the bean sprouts. Serve with rice, noodles or pasta.

Yield: 4 servings

HOSIN CHICKEN

2 chicken breasts, cut into
  ½-inch chunks
3 tablespoons Hosin sauce
5 scallions
8 asparagus spears
4 mushrooms

1 green bell pepper
2 yellow squash
  sesame oil
1 cup unsalted peanuts
1 to 2 chili peppers,
  broken up

Slice chicken into ½-inch pieces; place in bowl with Hosin sauce; coat and allow to marinate for at least ½ hour. Clean and chop scallions, asparagus, mushrooms, pepper and squash. Heat sesame oil in wok or large skillet; add marinated chicken and sauté along with crushed chili peppers. After chicken is browned, add the vegetables and stir-fry until done; approximately 3 to 5 minutes. Serve over rice.

Yield: 4 servings

CHICKEN CANZANESE

2 chickens (about 3 pounds each), cut into 8 serving pieces
1 tablespoon kosher salt
½ teaspoon sage
4 bay leaves
2 cloves garlic, sliced crosswise
12 whole cloves
3 sprigs fresh rosemary or 1 teaspoon dried
24 black peppercorns, crushed
¼ teaspoon dried red pepper flakes
4 slices prosciutto, ¼-inch thick, cut into ¼-inch dice
½ cup dry white vermouth
½ cup chopped fresh parsley to garnish

Put the chicken pieces in a large bowl. Sprinkle with the salt and cover with cold water. Let stand for 1 hour. Drain the chicken pieces and arrange in a single layer in a large flame-proof casserole. Add the sage, bay leaves, garlic, rosemary, black peppercorns, red pepper flakes, prosciutto and vermouth. Cover and cook over low heat for 1 hour. Remove the cover, increase the heat to moderately high and cook until the sauce is reduced and chicken colors. Serve with fresh parsley.

Yield: 8 servings

CHICKEN CRAB CASSEROLE

2 tablespoons chopped onion
½ cup butter
7 tablespoons all-purpose flour
1 teaspoon salt
1 teaspoon paprika
1 teaspoon crushed rosemary
2 cups chicken stock
2 cups sour half-and-half or sour cream
3 cups cubed cooked chicken
1 cup cooked flaked crab meat
1 large or 2 small avocados
1 tablespoon lemon juice
1 cup fresh bread crumbs
2 tablespoons butter
half bunch watercress to garnish

Melt the butter in a large saucepan and sauté the onion until golden. Add flour, salt, paprika and rosemary and cook, stirring until mixture bubbles. Gradually add chicken stock, stirring with a wire whisk until mixture comes to a boil. Remove from heat and stir in the sour half-and-half or sour cream. Add chicken and crab meat. Cut avocado into cubes and sprinkle with lemon juice. Blend gently into chicken mixture. Turn into a 2-quart baking dish and cover top evenly with bread crumbs which have been sautéed with 2 tablespoons butter. Bake at 350° for 30 minutes. Serve and garnish with watercress sprigs. May be frozen and reheated. If freezing, add avocado after thawing.

Yield: 6 servings

COLD CHICKEN BREASTS WITH GREEN SAUCE

Chicken:

6 boneless skinless chicken breast halves

½ cup bottled Italian vinaigrette dressing

2 tablespoons unsalted butter

Green Sauce:

½ cup mayonnaise

½ cup sour cream

¼ cup chopped spinach or other greens

2 tablespoons chopped green onions, including green parts

2 teaspoons fresh lemon juice

½ teaspoon tarragon

½ teaspoon basil

½ teaspoon marjoram

¼ teaspoon hot pepper sauce

salt

6 cherry tomatoes to garnish

Marinate chicken breasts in the vinaigrette dressing for about 30 minutes. In a large skillet, heat the butter until foaming. Lift the chicken breasts from the marinade, drain off excess marinade and place in skillet in one layer. Sauté over medium heat until breasts are cooked through and just lose their pinkness, turning several times. Do not overcook; it will take about 15 minutes for large, thick breast halves. When done, remove from skillet and cool. The chicken will be a golden brown. If not using immediately, cover and refrigerate. Bring to room temperature before serving.

To make the sauce, combine all the remaining ingredients except the tomatoes and mix well. Add salt to taste. To make tomato flowers, carefully slice ⅔ through the tomato being sure not to sever the halves. Make another slice at right angles. Open up "petals." Top with the green sauce and garnish with a tomato flower.

Yield: 6 servings

EASY ROAST DUCK WITH TOMATO RHUBARB SAUCE

Tomato Rhubarb Sauce:

3½ pounds tomatoes, peeled, seeded and chopped

4 stalks of rhubarb, trimmed and cut into 1-inch pieces

½ cup sugar

½ cup cider vinegar

3 tablespoons fresh ginger root, peeled and minced

Easy Roast Duck:

1 (4½ to 5½-pound) duck chicken or duck stock to cover

½ teaspoon coarse salt

¼ teaspoon freshly ground pepper

cilantro or other greens

To prepare the sauce, in a large saucepan combine the tomatoes, rhubarb, sugar, vinegar and ginger root. Bring to a boil and simmer for 1 hour, stirring occasionally.

To prepare the duck, cut into quarters and prick the skin all over with a fork. Heat the stock in a large saucepan to boiling, add the duck pieces carefully, and allow the stock to return to a boil. Reduce the heat and simmer the breast sections for 14 minutes, the leg sections for 20 minutes. Place skin side up, under a preheated broiler for about 6 minutes. Serve the sections on a bed of cilantro or other greens and top with the sauce.

Yield: 2 servings

BEEF TENDERLOIN WITH FOUR SAUCES

3 to 4 pounds beef
   tenderloin

choice of sauce

Preheat oven to 450°. Place beef in shallow pan and put into oven. After 5 minutes reduce oven temperature to 375°. Cook for 20 to 25 minutes. Meat will be very rare at 125° on a meat thermometer or medium rare at 135°. Let the meat stand for 10 minutes before carving. Serve with sauce of your choice.

Mustard Peppercorn Sauce:

1 tablespoon sugar
2 tablespoons tarragon
   vinegar
¼ cup Dijon mustard
½ teaspoon salt
2 egg yolks

2 tablespoons green
   peppercorns, rinsed and
   drained
1 tablespoon unsalted
   butter
½ cup heavy cream

In the top of a double boiler, combine the sugar, vinegar, mustard, salt, egg yolks and peppercorns. Whisk over hot water until thickened, about 5 minutes. Remove from heat and stir in butter. Set aside. Whip the cream until stiff and gently fold into the mustard base. Cover and refrigerate until serving time.

Goat Cheese Sauce:

4 ounces Montrachet-type
   goat cheese
2 tablespoons minced fresh
   parsley
1 small clove garlic, minced

¼ teaspoon freshly ground
   black pepper
4 tablespoons heavy cream
2 teaspoons sherry wine
   vinegar

In a small bowl, mix the ingredients together and set aside until ready to serve.

(Beef Tenderloin with Four Sauces, continued on next page)

(Beef Tenderloin with Four Sauces, continued)

Roquefort Sauce:

2 tablespoons unsalted butter

½ pound sliced mushrooms

½ cup dry sherry

⅔ cup heavy cream

½ cup Roquefort cheese

pinch of cayenne pepper (optional)

fresh minced parsley to garnish

Melt butter in a heavy skillet and sauté the mushrooms until tender. Remove the mushrooms and set aside. Pour off any liquid in pan. Deglaze the pan with sherry and then add the cream. Reduce sauce until it thickens slightly. Stir in Roquefort cheese; add the mushrooms and heat. Adjust seasonings, adding cayenne pepper if desired. Pour over meat and garnish with parsley.

Wasabi Butter:

¼ cup softened unsalted butter

2 tablespoons Wasabi powder, or to taste

2 tablespoons minced fresh parsley

Mix together butter and powder. Stir in parsley. Using waxed paper, form into cylinder. Chill for at least 1 hour. Place slice of butter on meat at serving time.

Yield: 4 to 6 servings

BEER MARINATED FLANK STEAK

1 to 2 bottles beer

6 green onions, minced

⅓ cup vegetable oil

2 tablespoons soy sauce

2 teaspoons Worcestershire sauce (optional)

2 tablespoons brown sugar

2 cloves garlic, minced

½ teaspoon ground ginger

1¾ to 2 pounds flank steak

In a large mixing bowl, combine all ingredients except steak; mix well. Add steak, coating it well with marinade; cover bowl. Refrigerate steak in marinade overnight or up to 3 days. Drain steak; grill to desired doneness. Cut across grain into thin slices and serve.

Yield: 4 to 6 servings

SHORT RIBS WITH COGNAC SAUCE

3	pounds beef short ribs	2	teaspoons instant coffee
	all-purpose flour	1	teaspoon sugar
½	cup butter	3	tablespoons whipping
1	tablespoon vegetable oil		cream
2	onions, chopped	1	teaspoon salt
1	(8-ounce) can tomato	½	teaspoon fresh ground
	sauce		pepper
1	(8-ounce) can Italian	1	tablespoon cognac
	tomatoes		freshly chopped parsley to
1	cup dry red wine		garnish

Coat meat with flour. Heat butter and oil in a Dutch oven. Add meat and brown well; remove from pan. Add onions and sauté until tender. Return meat to the pan and add tomato sauce, tomatoes, wine, coffee, sugar, cream, salt and pepper. Simmer, covered, 1½ hours. Remove from heat, cool and refrigerate until fat congeals on the top. (To speed this process, the dish may be placed in the freezer). Heat oven to 350°. Remove congealed fat and heat the Dutch oven until the contents bubble. Stir in cognac and place in the oven. Bake, uncovered, 30 minutes and garnish with parsley.

Yield: 4 servings

HERB ROAST WITH WINE SAUCE

Roast:

1 tablespoon vegetable oil
1 (3 to 3½-pound) eye of round roast
1 teaspoon oregano

1 teaspoon salt
½ teaspoon garlic powder
½ teaspoon paprika
½ teaspoon pepper

Sauce:

2 tablespoons olive oil
2 tablespoons butter
1 large yellow onion, thinly sliced
3 bell peppers - one each; red, yellow and orange, thinly sliced

1 pound can tomatoes, crushed, reserve juice
6 ounces beef bouillon
½ cup burgundy wine
½ cup cold coffee
½ teaspoon hot pepper sauce

To prepare roast, rub all over with oil. Combine oregano, salt, garlic powder, paprika and pepper and rub over surface of meat. Place fat side up in baking pan. Bake at 350° for 1 hour or 20 minutes per pound.

To prepare sauce, melt butter with oil and sauté onion and peppers in a skillet over medium high heat until soft. Place vegetables in a saucepan with all the other ingredients. Bring to boil over medium heat. Reduce heat and simmer until sauce is thickened, approximately 20 to 25 minutes. Pour sauce over sliced beef and serve.

Yield: 8 to 10 servings

TERIYAKI POT ROAST

1 (3 to 4-pound) blade pot
   roast
2 tablespoons all-purpose
   flour
½ teaspoon salt
⅛ teaspoon pepper
½ teaspoon curry powder
3 tablespoons vegetable oil

¼ cup water
¼ cup honey
¼ cup soy sauce
2 tablespoons chopped
   fresh ginger root or ½
   teaspoon ground ginger
¼ cup all-purpose flour
¼ cup sherry (optional)

In large mixing bowl, combine 2 tablespoons flour, salt, pepper and curry powder. Dredge meat in seasoned flour; brown meat in Dutch oven using vegetable oil; pour off drippings. Add water, soy sauce, honey, ginger and sherry; cover pan tightly. Cook over low heat 3 to 3½ hours until tender. If more gravy is desired, add ½ cup water and ½ cup sherry or 1 cup water. Continue cooking over low heat, adding flour to thicken for gravy. Serve with Oriental vegetables and rice.

Yield: 4 to 6 servings

STEAK ON TORTILLAS

1 (2 to 3-pound) steak
3 flour tortillas, large size
3 tomatoes, seeded and
   chopped
¼ cup chopped cilantro
   leaves

4 green onions, cut into
   ¼-inch slices
5 to 6 slices Monterey Jack
   cheese

Grill or broil steak to desired color. Put the uncooked flour tortillas on a platter. Cut up steak as desired and place it on the tortillas. Add tomatoes, cilantro and onions evenly over the steak. Cover all with cheese slices; broil until melted and heated thoroughly.

Yield: 6 servings

GERMAN STYLE BEEF BRISKET

1 medium onion, thinly
  sliced
1 clove garlic, thinly sliced
1 (4-pound) beef brisket,
  trimmed of fat
½ cup apple brandy
¼ cup raisins
1 medium cooking apple,
  finely chopped
2 tablespoons firmly packed
  brown sugar

1 tablespoon grated orange
  peel
1 tablespoon minced
  crystallized ginger
½ (1-ounce) package brown
  gravy mix
½ teaspoon cinnamon
½ teaspoon ground ginger
¼ teaspoon pepper

Arrange onion and garlic on bottom of 12 x 9-inch roasting pan. Add brisket. Cover and roast at 300° for 3 hours. Remove brisket; discard onion and garlic. Skim grease off pan juices. Add remaining ingredients and return brisket to pan. Cover and roast an additional 1½ hours. Transfer to platter; slice thinly and serve. Pass sauce separately.

Yield: 6 servings

MOUSSAKA

Vegetable Mixture:

2 (1-pound) eggplants
2 eggs

3 tablespoons vegetable oil
1 cup dry bread crumbs

Meat Sauce:

2 tablespoons vegetable oil
2 medium sized onions, finely chopped
1 clove garlic, minced
1½ pounds lean ground beef
1 (16-ounce) can tomatoes

1 tablespoon tomato paste
½ teaspoon oregano
½ teaspoon basil
½ teaspoon salt
¼ teaspoon ground black pepper

Egg Mixture:

4 large eggs
1 (8-ounce) container plain yogurt or sour cream

1 cup milk
½ cup freshly grated Parmesan cheese

To prepare vegetable mixture, preheat oven to 450°. Wash and dry eggplant. Slice into ½-inch thick rounds and soak in salted water for 30 minutes. Dry slices thoroughly. Beat 2 eggs with oil; dip eggplant in egg mixture, then in bread crumbs. Place on a greased baking sheet in a single layer. Bake in upper third of preheated oven at 450° for 10 minutes without turning.

To prepare meat sauce, place oil, onion, garlic and ground beef in a large skillet. Over medium high heat, cook until onions are soft and beef is browned. Drain off any fat. Add tomatoes, tomato paste, oregano, basil, salt and pepper. Bring all ingredients to a boil. Reduce heat and continue to simmer, uncovered, for 30 minutes. Season to taste.

To prepare egg mixture, with a wire whisk, beat 4 eggs and yogurt or sour cream to blend; add milk and mix well.

To assemble casserole, oil a 13 x 9 x 2-inch casserole dish. Layer ½ the eggplant on the bottom, overlapping if necessary. Spread ½ the meat sauce and top with ½ of egg mixture. Repeat the process with remaining ingredients. Sprinkle Parmesan cheese over top and bake in upper third of a preheated 350° oven for 30 minutes or until it is golden.

Yield: 8 servings

LAMB IN GINGERED CRANBERRY SAUCE

2	pounds cubed lean lamb	1	cup red burgundy
2	teaspoons seasoned salt	½	cup water
¼	teaspoon pepper	1	(16-ounce) can whole
¼	teaspoon garlic powder		cranberry sauce
½	cup diced onion	¼	teaspoon ground ginger
1	(6-ounce) can tomato	¼	teaspoon ground oregano
	paste		

In a large skillet, brown lamb; pour off fat. Add onion, seasonings, tomato paste, wine and water; cover and simmer 45 minutes. Add cranberry sauce and simmer an additional 45 minutes more. Serve hot over rice.

Yield: 4 to 6 servings

LAMB CHOPS WITH SORREL SAUCE

½	cup chicken stock	1⅓	cups dry white wine
½	cup heavy cream	5	ounces fresh sorrel leaves
4	tablespoons butter		or ¼ cup puréed sorrel
2	tablespoons olive oil		from a jar
8	rib lamb chops, (1-inch	½	cup chopped fresh mint
	thick)		fresh mint sprigs as
	salt and freshly ground		garnish
	pepper to taste		

In a medium saucepan bring the stock and cream to a boil over high heat, stirring occasionally and reduce the mixture to ½ cup. In a large skillet melt the butter and sauté the lamb chops, turning once until browned outside but still pink in the center (3 minutes each side for rare, 4 minutes for medium, 5 for well-done). Transfer to a platter, cover loosely and keep warm in low oven. Pour off and discard the fat from skillet; add the wine and bring mixture to a boil over high heat reducing by half. If using fresh sorrel, slice leaves into thin ribbons. Add sorrel and mint and cook for 1 minute. Add the reduced cream mixture and cook until sauce is hot. Season to taste with salt and pepper. Pour over chops and garnish with mint sprigs.

Yield: 4 servings

MARINATED GRILLED BUTTERFLIED LEG OF LAMB

Leg of Lamb:

1 (8 to 9-pound) leg of lamb, butterflied

salt and freshly ground pepper to taste

Marinade #1:

¼ cup olive oil
1 cup dry red wine
2 tablespoons Dijon mustard
2 tablespoons finely chopped garlic

2 teaspoons dried thyme or 4 sprigs fresh
1 crumbled bay leaf
1 teaspoon coriander
2 teaspoons dried rosemary or 4 sprigs fresh
2 tablespoons butter

Marinade #2:

¾ cup salad oil
⅓ cup fresh lemon juice
½ cup dry sherry
2 tablespoons minced Bermuda onion
2 teaspoons salt

1 teaspoon dried ground oregano
2 teaspoon finely crushed dried mint
3 heavy splashes hot pepper sauce

Preheat broiler or prepare charcoal grill. Lay lamb flat and sprinkle with salt and generous quantity of pepper on both sides.

For marinade #1, in a bowl combine all the remaining ingredients except the butter and blend them well. Place lamb in baking dish and pour marinade over it. Turn and rub marinade into lamb so it is evenly coated. It is not necessary to refrigerate before cooking but, if it has been, let it return to room temperature by allowing to sit for at least 1 hour. Remove lamb from marinade, reserving marinade. Place lamb flat on the grill approximately 5 to 6 inches from the coals. If a broiler is used, place the lamb 4 to 5 inches under it . Cook lamb 10 minutes. Turn and cook another 10 minutes for rare meat. Cook longer to taste if preference is medium or well-done meat. Transfer marinade to a saucepan and simmer for 3 minutes. Add butter. Transfer lamb to a baking dish and pour warmed marinade

(Marinated Grilled Butterflied Leg of Lamb, continued on next page)

(Marinated Grilled Butterflied Leg of Lamb, continued)

over it. Cover loosely with aluminum foil and let meat sit in a warm place for 10 to 15 minutes. Slice thinly and serve with pan gravy.

For marinade #2, mix all ingredients except lamb in a shallow pan. Cover and refrigerate lamb in marinade mixture overnight, turning a couple of times. Place on charcoal grill 6 inches from coals and baste with marinade. Cook for approximately 25 minutes on each side. May also be prepared under the broiler using the same times.

Yield: 6 to 8 servings

SWEDISH LEG OF LAMB

Leg of Lamb:

1 (5 to 5½) pound leg of lamb
1 clove garlic, slivered
1 tablespoon salt
1 teaspoon dry mustard

1 cup strong coffee
2 teaspoons sugar
2 teaspoons cream
1 ounce brandy

Gravy:

drippings from roast pan
5 tablespoons all-purpose flour

¾ cup heavy cream
2 tablespoons currant jelly

Preheat oven to 350°. Wipe leg of lamb with a damp cloth; jab surface with sharp pointed knife and insert slivers of garlic. Rub the meat with salt and dry mustard. Place in a roasting pan. Combine coffee, sugar, cream and brandy in a small bowl to use as marinade. After about 1¼ to 1½ hours baste all over with marinade. Continue to cook another 1¼ to 1½ hours. Total cooking time should be 2½ to 3 hours.

When roast is done, remove to platter and keep warm. Add flour to the drippings in the pan and stir until smooth. Stir in cream and currant jelly and cook until bubbling. Serve on the side with leg of lamb.

Yield: 4 to 6 servings

STUFFED BREAST OF LAMB

Stuffing:

1	pound Swiss chard, kale or celery cabbage	1	small onion, minced	
2	leeks	2	slices bread	
4	ounces ground pork stew meat	⅓	cup milk	
1	bunch parsley	1	clove garlic, minced	
		2	eggs	
			salt and pepper to taste	

Breast of Lamb:

1	7 pound breast of lamb, boned (2-3 pieces)	1	quart lamb or veal stock (beef stock may be substituted)
1	pound sliced bacon		
¾	cup dry white wine		

To make stuffing, cut chard, kale or cabbage into 1-inch pieces. Cut green part only of leeks into 1-inch pieces. Remove stems from parsley. Soak bread in milk for 5 minutes. Combine all above ingredients in blender or food processor and mix until stuffing is correct consistency.

Arrange lamb cut side up on work surface, overlapping short ends slightly. Spread stuffing over lamb leaving 1-inch border. Roll lamb up jelly roll fashion starting at one long side. Wrap with bacon slices and tie with kitchen twine to hold shape. Transfer to roasting pan. Roast lamb at 450° for 45 minutes. Add wine, scraping up any browned bits from bottom of roasting pan. Pour in stock. Turn lamb over and cover pan with foil. Roast an additional hour. When done, transfer lamb to serving platter. Let stand for 10 minutes before slicing. Degrease pan juices and serve over lamb slices.

Yield: 8 servings

LAMB ROASTED WITH SAUERKRAUT

2	pounds sauerkraut	1	cup chicken stock
½	cup vegetable oil	¼	cup pitted Greek olives
2	bay leaves	1	cup sour cream
2	teaspoons onion salt	1	cup chopped parsley
½	teaspoon pepper	1	cup fresh chopped dill
1	small leg of lamb	4	to 6 cloves garlic, minced

Preheat oven to 350°. Drain sauerkraut; place in a bowl. Pour boiling water over it; stir and drain. Repeat process once more. Place sauerkraut in a large skillet with the oil, bay leaves, onion salt and pepper. Cover and cook over low heat stirring occasionally until golden brown. Place lamb in roasting pan with a lid. Cover lamb with stock. Cover meat with sauerkraut and olives. Cover and bake in a preheated 350° oven for 1¼ hours. Add sour cream, parsley, dill and garlic and stir. Cover and bake 15 minutes more.

Yield: 4 to 6 servings

BARBECUED PORK WITH VEGETABLES

4	small barbecued pork back ribs	2	stalks of celery
2	small yellow squash	10	spinach leaves
2	medium carrots	3	small dried chilies, crushed
4	scallions		bean sprouts
6	sprigs cilantro		pepper to taste

Bone ribs and slice pork into ½-inch pieces. Julienne carrots, squash and scallions. Coarsely chop cilantro and spinach. Thinly slice celery. Place all vegetables in a large mixing bowl and crush small dried chilies over vegetables. Heat oil in wok or large frying pan. Add vegetables, stir. Add pepper and stir again. Add pork, stir until thoroughly heated. Serve over hot brown rice and top with sprouts.

Yield: 4 servings

PORK CHOPS WITH GIN

4	loin pork chops	1	large orange, zest
¼	cup all-purpose flour		removed and juice
½	teaspoon salt		extracted
¼	teaspoon pepper	½	cup fresh orange juice
1	tablespoon corn oil	½	cup gin
1	clove garlic, crushed	¼	cup chopped parsley

Dredge 4 loin pork chops in flour seasoned with salt and pepper. Sauté the chops in a large skillet until they are brown on both sides. Sprinkle with the garlic and orange zest and pour the orange juice and gin over them. Cook, covered, over low heat, turning occasionally, until they are tender, about ½ hour. The sauce will have cooked down and thickened. Sprinkle with parsley and serve with sauce and rice.

Yield: 4 servings

PORK CHOPS WITH APPLES AND ONIONS

6	loin pork chops, 1-inch thick	¾	cup all-purpose flour
		1	large red onion
½	teaspoon salt	4	tart apples
¼	pound butter	¼	cup brown sugar

Preheat oven to 250°. Salt pork chops on both sides. Melt butter in large frying pan. Flour pork chops on both sides and place chops in frying pan and brown on both sides. Transfer pork chops to baking dish. Place sliced onion rings on top of each chop. Peel, core and slice apples. Place apple rings on top of onions and sprinkle with brown sugar. Cover and bake for 15 minutes. Reduce heat to 200° and bake for 30 minutes more.

Yield: 3 to 4 servings

PORK CHOPS WITH PEARS

6 pork chops, about 1-inch thick, trimmed of all fat thyme, salt and pepper to taste
3 tablespoons butter
1 small onion, chopped
3 tablespoons fresh lemon juice
3 tablespoons orange juice
½ cup dry sherry

1 tablespoon brown sugar
¼ teaspoon ground ginger
1 tablespoon cornstarch
3 medium red Bartlett pears, cored, cut into 1-inch slices
1 cup dried tart cherries or blueberries or combination you prefer

Sprinkle chops with salt, pepper and thyme. Heat butter in a large skillet; add chops. Cook until brown on both sides, turning once. Remove chops. Add onion to skillet. Cook and stir until brown. Add chops, 1 cup water, lemon juice, orange juice, sherry, sugar and ginger. Heat to boil. Simmer, covered, for 30 minutes or until chops are tender. Dissolve cornstarch in ¼ cup water. Stir into mixture. Cook and stir until thickened. Add pears and mixed fruits. Cook and stir 2 minutes. Serve with rice or noodles.

Yield: 6 servings

PORK ROAST WITH LIME

4 pounds pork loin
3 large cloves garlic, sliced
1 tablespoon dried oregano
⅓ cup fresh lime juice

½ teaspoon freshly ground pepper
1½ teaspoons salt

In a bowl just large enough to hold the pork, combine the garlic, oregano, lime juice and pepper. Add the pork, cover, and let it marinate in the refrigerator overnight, turning occasionally. Bring pork to room temperature. Discard the marinade and transfer the pork to a roasting pan. Season pork with salt. Cover loosely with foil and roast at 350° for 1 hour, uncover and roast for 1½ hours more. Remove to platter and let stand for 10 minutes before carving. Serve with rice and black beans.

Yield: 10 to 12 servings

PORK TENDERLOIN

2   (6-ounce) jars currant
    jelly
2   (6-ounce) jars water
    juice of 1 lemon
½   teaspoon allspice

dash Worcestershire
    sauce
1   onion, chopped
2   pork tenderloins

Heat jelly, water, lemon juice, allspice and Worcestershire sauce until jelly is melted. Using a shallow roasting pan, put onion on the tenderloins. Put half the sauce on the meat. Save the remaining sauce for basting and/or to serve at the table. Bake, uncovered, for 1 hour at 350°.

Yield: 6 servings

SWEET AND SOUR PORK

3   pounds pork, cut into
    1-inch cubes
⅔   cup brown sugar
2   tablespoons cornstarch
2   teaspoons dry mustard
⅔   cup vinegar
1   cup pineapple chunks,
    undrained

½   cup ketchup
½   cup water
2   tablespoons soy sauce
3   green peppers, chopped
    into 1-inch pieces
1   large onion, chopped

Brown pork and place in casserole. In a large pan, combine other ingredients except peppers and onion. Cook over medium heat until thick and smooth. Pour over pork. Bake at 350° for 1½ hours. Stir in peppers and onion and cook for 15 more minutes.

Yield: 6 to 8 servings

VEAL AND PORK WITH RICE CASSEROLE

1 onion, chopped	½ pound mushrooms, sliced
2 cups chopped celery	½ cup wild rice
1 pound cubed veal	½ cup white rice
½ pound cubed pork	2 tablespoons soy sauce
1 clove garlic	3 to 4 cups beef stock
3 tablespoons butter	

Brown onion, celery, meat and garlic in 1½ tablespoons butter. In separate pan sauté mushrooms in remaining butter; mix with meat mixture. Add rices and soy sauce. Place in a 13 x 9 x 2-inch casserole dish. Cover with 3 cups of beef stock. Cover and bake in a 350° oven for 2 hours. After 1 hour, check casserole; if dry add more beef stock.

Yield: 6 servings

VEAL MARSALA

1 pound veal scallops	1 pound fresh asparagus
flour	10 ounces grated Fontinella
salt and pepper to taste	cheese
4 tablespoons butter	⅓ cup Marsala wine
3 tablespoons vegetable oil	

Pound veal between pieces of waxed paper. Dredge veal in flour seasoned with salt and pepper. Brown in 2 tablespoons of butter and 3 tablespoons of oil. Line a 11 x 7-inch baking pan with foil; place browned veal in the bottom and cover with asparagus. Salt and pepper to taste. Cover with the grated cheese. Pour Marsala wine into the pan used to brown the veal; cook for 1 minute, scraping the browned bits off the bottom of the pan. Add remaining 2 tablespoons of butter and melt; pour sauce over the veal and asparagus. Cover pan tightly with foil and bake in a 400° oven for 20 minutes.

Yield: 4 servings

SHRIMP IN PERNOD SAUCE

1¼ pounds shrimp or bay
     scallops
8 tablespoons butter
2 tablespoons shallots
¾ ounce Pernod
5 cloves garlic, minced

4 ounces dry white wine
4 ounces fish stock
1 cup whipping cream
1 tablespoon tarragon
   salt and pepper

Melt 3 tablespoons butter. Add the shrimp (or scallops) and shallots. Add Pernod and ignite. Add the garlic and wine; simmer 2 minutes. Remove the shrimp. Reduce the sauce by ⅓. Add the stock and reduce the sauce by ½. Add the cream and tarragon and cook until the sauce thickens. Add the shrimp and serve.

Yield: 4 servings

SHRIMP IN BEER CREOLE

½ cup sliced blanched
   almonds
3 tablespoons butter
1 tablespoon oil
2 pounds shrimp, shelled
   and deveined
¼ cup butter (½ stick)
¼ cup minced scallions

1 green pepper, sliced
½ pound small mushrooms
1 tablespoon paprika
1 teaspoon tomato paste
1 cup light beer
¾ cup heavy cream
¼ cup sour cream
   salt and pepper to taste

In small skillet, sauté blanched almonds in 1 tablespoon each of butter and oil, tossing until golden brown. Drain on paper towels and sprinkle with salt. Set aside. In saucepan, cook shrimp in ¼ cup butter over moderate heat; tossing until just pink. Transfer shrimp and pan juices to a bowl and set aside. Add 2 tablespoons butter to the pan and sauté scallions and green pepper cut into slices, until they are soft. Add mushrooms, paprika and salt and pepper to taste. Toss mixture until mushrooms are tender. Stir in tomato paste, light beer and the reserved pan juices and reduce the liquid over high heat to ½ cup. Reduce heat to low; add heavy cream combined with sour cream and the reserved shrimp and simmer until hot. Serve garnished with almonds.

Yield: 6 servings

SPICED SHRIMP

1 pound large shrimp, shelled and deveined	3 whole cloves
	salt and pepper
3 tablespoons olive oil	¼ teaspoon grated nutmeg
½ teaspoon ground cinnamon	¼ cup rum
	¼ cup lemon juice

Sauté shrimp in oil until just pink. Remove from heat. Stir in cinnamon, whole cloves, salt and pepper; grate nutmeg over the shrimp. Let steep, covered, 30 minutes or more. When ready to serve, reheat shrimp and warm rum. Flame rum and pour over shrimp in pan and stir. Squeeze on lemon juice and serve.

Yield: 4 servings

BARBECUED FISH WITH RED PEPPER CREAM

Barbecued Fish:

2 pounds of firm-fleshed fish fillets, (halibut, albacore, swordfish), cut 1½ inch thick	3 tablespoons fresh lemon juice
	¼ cup minced fresh cilantro
¼ cup olive oil	1 clove garlic, minced
	¼ teaspoon salt

Red Pepper Cream:

2 large red bell peppers	2 tablespoons fresh lemon juice
1 jalapeño pepper	
2 large cloves garlic	1 cup olive oil
2 egg yolks	

Combine oil, lemon juice, cilantro, garlic and salt. Whisk until thickened and well combined. Pour over the fish and marinate for 4 to 6 hours. Barbecue for 10 minutes for each inch of thickness, turning half way through the cooking time. Serve with red pepper cream.

Seed and dice bell and jalapeño peppers. In a food processor, combine the pepper, jalapeño, garlic, egg yolks and lemon juice. Process until very smooth. Slowly pour in oil in a steady stream. Will keep for 7 to 10 days in the refrigerator.

Yield: 6 servings

TROUT WITH LEMONGRASS

1 (1-pound) trout, cleaned with head and tail intact	¼ cup butter
6 (6-inch) lengths of fresh lemongrass	½ cup mayonnaise
salt and pepper	1 teaspoon chopped chives
flour	1 teaspoon fresh lemon juice

Wash the fish and pat dry. Lay the pieces of lemongrass in the cavity of the fish; sprinkle the fish with salt and pepper and dust it with flour. Melt the butter in a heavy skillet. Add the trout and sauté it over moderate heat for 5 minutes on each side, or until it is browned and flakes easily when tested with a fork. Skin and fillet the trout quickly. Arrange it on plates and cover each fillet with mayonnaise, which has been seasoned with lemon juice and chives. Serve immediately.

Yield: 2 servings

SNAPPER IMPERIAL

4 (6-ounce) snapper fillets	salt, pepper, cayenne pepper to taste
12 ounces fresh back-fin crabmeat	1 cup heavy cream
2 tablespoons butter	5 egg whites
¼ cup dry vermouth	3 teaspoons lemon juice
4 teaspoons flour	black caviar to garnish (optional)

Sauté crab in butter and vermouth; add flour and seasonings to taste. Add cream; cook until thickened. Beat egg whites. Broil snapper for 2 to 3 minutes until almost done. Combine lemon juice, salt and pepper and pour over fish. Cover fish with crabmeat, top with egg whites. Bake at 500° for 2 to 5 minutes until egg whites are lightly browned. If desired, garnish with caviar.

Yield: 4 servings

SALT COD WITH FIGS

Salt Cod:

1½ pounds salt codfish
1½ cups milk
  1 tablespoon chopped
    peeled fresh ginger
  1 2-inch strip lemon peel

3 tablespoons butter
1 tablespoon flour
1 clove garlic, crushed
1 roasted red pepper
  salt and pepper to taste

Baked Fresh Figs:

  6 ripe figs
  ½ teaspoon orange-flower
    water or Cointreau

  water
2 tablespoons sliced toasted
  almonds

Soak salt cod in cold water for 12 hours, changing the water every three hours. Drain the fish and place in a saucepan and cover with fresh cold water. Bring gently to a boil and simmer for 15 minutes or until it is tender. Drain thoroughly on paper towels. Remove skin and bones and flake the fish. Scald the milk with the ginger and lemon peel. Let the milk cool and strain it. In a saucepan, melt 1 tablespoon of the butter. Blend in flour and gradually add the strained milk, stirring until the sauce is smooth. In a skillet, melt the remaining 2 tablespoons butter and the garlic. Brown garlic well and discard after browning. Peel, seed and chop red pepper. Add the flaked fish and red pepper; heat mixture. Stir in the sauce and cook for about 3 minutes. Season with salt and pepper to taste.

Prick figs in several places with the tines of a fork. Arrange in a buttered baking dish. Sprinkle with water and seasoning. Bake at 300° for 15 minutes or until tender. Cut figs in half and arrange in a baking dish, cut side up. Cover with the fish mixture. Sprinkle with almonds and brown lightly under the broiler. Add almonds before serving with rice. Dish may be prepared ahead and reheated at 350° for about 20 minutes.

Yield: 6 servings

FISH WITH CHEVRE

6 to 8 fillets of snapper, orange roughy, sole or cod
3 tablespoons minced shallots
2 teaspoons minced fresh parsley
2 teaspoons minced fresh tarragon
4 to 6 tablespoons melted unsalted butter
½ cup heavy cream
6 to 8 ounces crumbled Chevre or other goat cheese
2 bunches fresh chopped, cooked and drained spinach or Swiss chard or combination of the two
½ cup minced green onions salt and pepper to taste

Preheat oven to 400°. In 1 tablespoon of the butter, sauté the shallots, parsley and tarragon until soft; about 3 minutes. Add the cream and simmer until slightly thickened. Add the cheese and heat, stirring constantly, until the cheese is melted and sauce is smooth. Remove from heat and cover. In 1 tablespoon of butter, sauté the onions; combine onions with cooked spinach or chard and spread over the bottom of a buttered baking dish. Arrange the fillets on top of the spinach. Brush with the remaining butter and season with salt and pepper. Cover with foil and bake for 12 to 15 minutes until fish is just done. Remove from oven and layer Chevre sauce over the fillets. Broil for 2 to 3 minutes until sauce is bubbly. Serve immediately.

Yield: 6 servings

ALASKAN STYLE SALMON

4 (6 to 8-ounce) Alaskan King Salmon fillets
4 tablespoons brown sugar
2 tablespoons dill
4 tablespoons butter salt or seasoned salt

Place 2 long sheets of foil on broiler pan. Rinse salmon and place skin side down on foil. Sprinkle with brown sugar and dill; dot with butter; salt lightly. Wrap and seal foil around fish. Bake at 350° for 15 minutes. Double the amount of brown sugar and dill for a more intense flavor.

Yield: 4 servings

SALMON IN PARCHMENT

Mornay Sauce:

3 tablespoons butter
¼ cup all-purpose flour
2 cups milk

4 ounces shredded Swiss or
   Gruyère cheese
¼ teaspoon nutmeg
   salt and pepper to taste

Salmon:

6 (6-ounce) salmon fillets
18 medium shrimp, shelled
   and deveined (optional)

2 julienned carrots
2 julienned celery stalks
½ cup chopped dill

To make the sauce, melt butter in a saucepan. Add flour and mix to make a paste. Heat until bubbly. Gradually add milk and cook until thickened. Remove from heat and stir in cheese until melted. Add nutmeg and salt and pepper, to taste. Refrigerate.

To make the salmon, cut parchment paper into 6 (14-inch) squares. Fold on the diagonal. Place 1 fillet in each piece of parchment, leaving one edge of salmon on the fold line. Place ⅙ of the carrots and celery on each fillet. Arrange 3 shrimp on top of vegetables. Sprinkle each with dill. Spoon several tablespoons of sauce on top of shrimp. Fold parchment paper over the top. Fold the edges over 2 or 3 times and staple around the 2 folded sides so that paper forms a secure triangular sack. May be stored on a cookie sheet in the refrigerator if made in advance. Bring to room temperature before baking. Bake in a 350° oven for 25 to 30 minutes. Remove from parchment sack and serve on individual plates.

Yield: 6 servings

SEAFOOD STRUDEL

2   tablespoons unsalted
    butter
2   tablespoons all-purpose
    flour
½   teaspoon Dijon mustard
    salt
    cayenne pepper
¾   cup milk at room
    temperature
2   tablespoons whipping
    cream
1   cup bread crumbs
¼   cup freshly grated
    Parmesan
¼   teaspoon dry mustard
½   pound cleaned shelled
    cooked shrimp
½   pound cleaned shelled
    cooked crabmeat

½   pound cooked halibut (or
    any firm fish), cut into
    bite-size chunks
½   pound phyllo pastry
    sheets
¾   cup grated Swiss cheese
2   hard boiled eggs, chopped
¾   cup sour cream
¼   cup parsley
¼   cup diced shallots
2   tablespoons chopped
    chives
1   large clove garlic, minced
¾   cup melted unsalted
    butter
2   tablespoons chopped
    parsley
2   tablespoons freshly grated
    Parmesan cheese
    minced parsley to garnish

In a small saucepan, melt 2 tablespoons butter over low heat. Stir in flour to make smooth paste; heat gently, stirring constantly, until mixture just begins to bubble. Remove from heat and add Dijon mustard, pinch of salt and cayenne pepper. Slowly stir in milk. Cook over medium heat, stirring constantly until mixture bubbles and thickens. Add cream and adjust seasonings to taste. Cover and chill until thick and firm, about 2 hours. Preheat oven to 375°. Butter baking sheet. Combine bread crumbs, Parmesan cheese and dry mustard in a small bowl. Layer seafood evenly on phyllo and sprinkle with Swiss cheese and chopped egg. Dot with sour cream. Sprinkle with parsley, shallots, chives and garlic and dot with chilled sauce. Roll as directed on phyllo package. Place on prepared baking sheet and brush with some of the melted butter. Bake for 12 minutes. Remove from oven and brush with more melted butter. Slice diagonally with serrated knife into 1½-inch

(Seafood Strudel, continued on next page)

(Seafood Strudel, continued)

pieces. Push slices together to reshape loaf. Add parsley to remaining butter and brush again. Return to oven and continue baking for 35 to 40 minutes more, until crisp and golden brown. Repeat brushing 3 more times during baking, reserving a little butter to brush on just before serving. Remove strudel from oven and brush with remaining butter. Cool 10 minutes before serving. Dust with Parmesan cheese and minced parsley.

Yield: 6 to 8 servings

SCALLOPS WITH TOMATOES

1¼ pounds scallops (use sea scallops if possible), cut in half	2 cups chopped, peeled and seeded tomatoes
¼ cup milk	2 tablespoons red wine vinegar
¼ cup flour, seasoned with salt and pepper to taste	2 tablespoons vegetable oil
2 tablespoons olive oil	½ cup chopped parsley or basil
3 teaspoons chopped garlic	

Soak scallops in milk and let stand for 15 minutes. Drain scallops and dredge in flour mixture. Shake scallops in colander or sieve to remove excess flour. Separate scallops on wax paper so they do not stick together. Sauté garlic and tomatoes in olive oil. Add the vinegar and simmer for 2 minutes. Heat vegetable oil in a non-stick skillet, large enough to hold all the scallops. Add scallops and cook until lightly browned (about 4 minutes). Pour sauce over scallops. Correct seasonings. Serve with rice or angel hair pasta.

Yield: 4 servings

SALTY DOG SCALLOPS

3 tablespoons unsalted butter
1 tablespoon olive oil
2 pounds scallops
1 teaspoon dried thyme
¼ teaspoon freshly ground pepper

⅓ cup vodka
½ cup fresh pink grapefruit juice
1 large pink grapefruit, peeled and sectioned
fresh thyme to garnish

In a heavy skillet, melt butter with oil. Sauté scallops sprinkling with thyme and pepper as they cook. When cooked, remove scallops to a platter and keep warm. Add the vodka to the pan and boil rapidly for 1 minute. Add the grapefruit juice and continue to boil until sauce is slightly thickened and reduced by about ⅓. Return the scallops to the pan. Add the grapefruit sections and cook over medium heat until warmed through. Garnish with fresh thyme.

Yield: 4 to 6 servings

SIDE DISHES

W.O. KERFOOTS BLOCK
FIRST IN THE BURNT DISTRICT

W.D. KERFOOT
ALL GONE BUT WIFE & CHILDREN
AND ENERGY

Immediately after the fire, Chicago rushed back
to "business as usual". This wooden shed for
Kerfoot Real Estate was erected within 48 hours.

SIDE DISHES

CAULIFLOWER WITH VANILLA SAUCE

3	tablespoons butter	2½	teaspoons vanilla
3	tablespoons flour	1	teaspoon fresh lemon juice
2	cups chicken stock		freshly ground pepper
1	tablespoon chicken-flavor soup base		salt, if needed
2	egg yolks	1	(2-pound) head of cauliflower
½	cup whipping cream		paprika to garnish
2	tablespoons minced fresh parsley		

Melt butter in a heavy medium saucepan. Add flour and cook until bubbly. Whisk in stock and soup base concentrate. Stir constantly until thickened and smooth. Whisk yolks and cream in a bowl. Add cream mixture, drop by drop, to thickened sauce, stirring constantly and adding more quickly toward the end until incorporated. Cook 1 minute, still stirring. Mix in parsley, vanilla, lemon juice, salt and pepper to taste. Can be prepared ahead and reheated. Rinse head of cauliflower and remove leaves and tough core. Wrap in micro-plastic or put in plastic bag; microwave on high for 6 minutes. Do not add water before wrapping (or cauliflower can be steamed crisp-tender for about 30 minutes). Serve cauliflower whole, covered with some of the sauce, the rest served separately, or serve individually, garnishing with sauce and a little paprika.

Yield: 6 servings

LEEK AND ONION AU GRATIN

1 slice whole wheat bread	½ cup chopped chives
1 cup grated mozzarella cheese	½ teaspoon oregano
	½ teaspoon basil
1 cup grated Monterey Jack cheese	½ teaspoon tarragon
	¼ teaspoon salt
4 cups sliced leeks, white only	⅛ teaspoon pepper
	½ cup vermouth
6 cups sliced medium onions	

Put bread in blender to make bread crumbs. Combine cheeses with bread crumbs. In a separate bowl combine all remaining ingredients except vermouth. Spread ½ onion mixture in a 13 x 9 x 2-inch baking dish. Top with cheese mixture. Repeat layers. Pour vermouth over top. Bake in a 350° oven for 1 hour.

Yield: 8 servings

ASPARAGUS WITH WARM TOMATO VINAIGRETTE

1 pound steamed crisp-tender asparagus	1 (16-ounce) can chopped peeled tomatoes or fresh tomatoes cooked, peeled and chopped with a healthy tablespoon of tomato paste added if tomatoes are not ripe
¼ cup chopped shallots or green onions	
¼ cup olive oil	
	1 clove garlic, minced
	⅔ cup dry vermouth
	pepper to taste

Steam asparagus. Keep warm. Combine other ingredients and heat over medium flame until hot. Stir frequently to prevent scorching. Pour sauce over vegetables and serve.

Yield: 4 servings

FIDDLEHEAD FERNS WITH BRUSSELS SAUCE

Fiddleheads:

1 pound fiddleheads, trimmed to 2-inch stems and carefully rinsed

1½ tablespoons butter
salt

Brussels Sauce:

2 large egg yolks
2 tablespoons fresh lemon juice
3 tablespoons finely chopped parsley

3 grinds fresh nutmeg
4 grinds fresh black pepper
¾ cup butter, melted
1 teaspoon salt

To prepare fiddleheads, carefully rinse and reshape heads to a tight curl if necessary. Bring a pot of salted water to a boil and drop in fiddleheads. Blanch for 1 minute, drain, and squeeze dry in a towel and reform heads. Melt butter in a large skillet and when cool, add the fiddleheads and set aside.

To prepare sauce, put egg yolks, 2 tablespoons lemon juice, parsley, nutmeg, pepper and salt into work bowl of a food processor and run for about 20 seconds. While running, add butter through feed tube. Run a few seconds longer. Transfer sauce to a small heavy saucepan and adjust seasoning after tasting. When ready to serve, whisk sauce over very low heat until just warm. Do not allow it to boil. Quickly reheat the fiddleheads in the skillet, tossing in the butter. Pour over the Brussels Sauce and serve.

Yield: 4 servings

CELERY PURÉE WITH RUM

3 large ribs celery, chopped
1 inner heart of celery with leaves, chopped
2 baking potatoes, peeled, cut into 1-inch squares
  salt and freshly ground pepper
2 tablespoons strong chicken stock made with chicken-flavored soup stock concentrate

1 tablespoon butter
1 tablespoon light rum
⅓ cup whipping cream
  chopped fresh parsley to garnish
  chopped fresh tarragon to garnish
  salt and pepper to taste

Place celery, celery heart and potatoes in a saucepan of boiling water seasoned with salt and pepper. Cook until tender, about 20 minutes; drain. Place vegetables in a food processor or blender and add chicken stock. (If using blender, add cream.) Purée until smooth. Place purée in a saucepan over low heat; stir in butter, rum and cream. Cook, stirring for about 3 minutes. Taste and add more salt and pepper to taste; garnish with parsley and tarragon. Serve hot.

Yield: 4 to 6 servings

BAKED FRENCH VEGETABLE CASSEROLE

16 to 20 small fresh onions, peeled and left whole
24 to 30 raw potato balls or cubes
2 cups shredded carrots
1 green pepper, cored, seeded and diced
¼ teaspoon ground cloves

¼ teaspoon salt
⅛ teaspoon pepper
½ pound butter
1 teaspoon sugar
1 teaspoon fresh lemon juice
2 cloves garlic, peeled and minced

Combine first 7 ingredients and put them in a large buttered casserole. In a saucepan, melt the butter and add the sugar, lemon juice and garlic. Pour the sauce over the vegetables in the casserole; cover tightly. Bake at 325° for 1 hour.

Yield: 6 servings

BAKED JERUSALEM ARTICHOKES

3 tablespoons olive oil
2 pounds Jerusalem
   artichokes, scrubbed and
   peeled
4 tablespoons unsalted
   butter, melted

1 tablespoon fresh lemon
   juice
   salt
   freshly ground pepper
¼ cup chopped parsley
½ cup sour cream

Preheat oven to 400°. Pour oil into a 13 x 9 x 2-inch baking pan and tilt to distribute oil over the bottom. Arrange artichokes in pan. Pour butter over artichokes; sprinkle with lemon juice, salt and pepper. Bake, uncovered, until artichokes are browned and tender, about 30 minutes for small artichokes; up to 60 minutes for large ones. Remove from oven, sprinkle with parsley and serve with a dollop of sour cream.

Yield: 8 servings

BAKED CABBAGE WITH GARLIC, JUNIPER AND CHEESE

8 whole juniper berries
2 large cloves garlic
½ teaspoon salt
2 tablespoons olive oil

2 pounds cabbage, finely
   sliced
½ cup grated Fontina
   cheese

Preheat oven to 425°. Using mortar and pestle, mash juniper berries, garlic and salt in mortar to a smooth paste, or mash ingredients to a paste in a bowl with the back of a spoon. Heat oil in a large heavy ovenproof casserole dish over medium heat. Stir in paste. Add cabbage and stir until completely coated. Sprinkle with cheese. Transfer to oven; bake for 15 minutes. Serve immediately.

Yield: 4 to 6 servings

BROCCOLI WITH STUFFING AND WALNUTS

1 large bunch fresh broccoli	1½ cups chicken stock
3 quarts boiling water	salt and pepper to taste
4 tablespoons butter	1 cup prepared herb
3 tablespoons all-purpose	stuffing mix
flour	1 cup coarsely chopped
1 tablespoon chicken stock	walnuts
concentrate from a jar	2 tablespoons butter

Trim and peel the broccoli. Cut the tops off the broccoli into 4-inch lengths. Cut the remaining stems on the diagonal into ⅜-inch slices. Total should equal approximately 4 cups of broccoli. Plunge the broccoli into boiling water and cook until crisp; about 5 minutes. Drain, rinse under cold water and drain again on paper towels. Melt 4 tablespoons butter in a large saucepan and add the flour. Cook until bubbly, stirring constantly; about 1 minute. Stir in chicken stock base and chicken stock, combine with a wire whisk to remove lumps and cook until sauce is smooth and thick. Place broccoli in a shallow baking pan. Sprinkle with stuffing mix. Melt 2 tablespoons butter in a skillet; stir in walnuts. Cook 2 or 3 minutes until lightly browned. Pour sauce over the broccoli and top with the walnuts. When ready to serve, bake the broccoli at 350° for about 20 minutes or until bubbling.

Yield: 6 servings

EGGPLANT CASSEROLE

½ pound ground beef
½ pound ground sausage
½ cup chopped onion
½ clove garlic, minced
2 (8-ounce) cans tomato
   sauce
⅛ teaspoon ground oregano

⅛ teaspoon basil leaves
1 large eggplant
2 beaten eggs
½ cup vegetable oil
½ pound mozzarella cheese,
   sliced or shredded

Sauté beef, sausage, onion and garlic until browned; pour off excess fat. Add tomato sauce, oregano and basil. Simmer while preparing eggplant. Peel and slice eggplant into thin slices, dip into beaten egg and sauté in oil until golden brown on both sides. Arrange eggplant, cheese and meat sauce in layers in a shallow 2-quart casserole, ending with cheese. Bake at 350° for 30 minutes or until bubbly and cheese has melted. All ground beef may be used instead of half beef and half sausage.

Yield: 4 to 6 servings

STIR-FRIED EGGPLANT PARMESAN

1 medium eggplant, peeled
   and cut in ½-inch cubes
1 teaspoon salt
¼ cup olive oil
¼ cup minced onion
2 tablespoons chopped
   green pepper
3 tablespoons chopped
   fresh basil

1 clove garlic, minced
¼ teaspoon rosemary
4 medium tomatoes, seeded
   and cubed
½ pound shredded
   mozzarella cheese
½ cup grated imported
   Romano cheese

Place eggplant in a colander and sprinkle with salt. Let stand 30 minutes to drain. Pat dry with paper towels. In a large skillet, add oil to coat the bottom. Heat before adding onion, green pepper, basil, garlic and rosemary. Stir for 3 minutes. Add eggplant and continue to stir-fry until lightly browned. Add tomatoes and stir-fry 1 minute more. Remove from heat and add cheeses, stirring to incorporate. Turn onto heated platter and serve.

Yield: 4 servings

FENNEL WITH TOMATOES AND CHEESE

2   large fennel bulbs (about
    1½-pounds after stem
    removal)
½   cup strong chicken stock
4   plum tomatoes
¼   cup olive oil

¼   cup freshly grated
    Parmesan or Romano
    cheese
1   tablespoon chopped fresh
    sage, basil or parsley
    salt and freshly ground
    pepper to taste

Trim the fennel bulbs of the discolored base, any bruised areas and the stems, if still attached. Cut each bulb lengthwise into ⅜-inch slices. In a large skillet, heat the stock to boiling and sauté the fennel slices over moderate heat until tender. Most of the stock will have been absorbed. Remove from heat. Arrange the slices, slightly overlapping, in a baking dish that will fit under the broiler. Cut the plum tomatoes in half lengthwise and arrange them, cut side up, around the fennel slices. Brush all with olive oil. Broil for about 5 minutes until heated. Sprinkle all with the cheese; broil 1 minute longer until cheese is lightly browned. Remove from broiler; sprinkle with fresh herbs, salt and ground pepper. Serve hot.

Yield: 4 servings

CHILLED MARINATED PEPPERS

8   large red, yellow or
    orange peppers (or
    combination)
3   tablespoons safflower oil
1   tablespoon olive oil
2   cloves garlic

1   tablespoon tarragon wine
    vinegar
½   teaspoon basil
¼   teaspoon rosemary
¼   teaspoon oregano

Skin peppers by placing them under broiler on foil-lined baking sheet. Turn peppers 2 or 3 times until skin blisters and turns black on all sides. Remove and place peppers in paper bag with top loosely folded. Cool for 1 hour. Slice into strips after removing seeds, stem and skin. Combine remaining ingredients and pour over peppers. Chill 24 to 48 hours. Serve with grilled beef or chicken.

Yield: 6 to 8 servings

OKRA WITH HOT SAUCE

1½ pounds okra
2 egg yolks
1 tablespoon Dijon mustard
2 tablespoons lemon juice
dash of hot pepper sauce

½ cup frozen unsalted
butter, cut into 5 pieces
1 tablespoon chopped fresh
basil or 1 teaspoon dried
salt and white pepper

Trim off the small, tough top of the okra cap, taking care not to cut into the green part of the cap. Drop okra into boiling, salted water and cook for 4 to 5 minutes, being careful not to overcook. Drain and keep warm. Combine egg yolks, mustard, lemon juice and hot pepper sauce in a small heavy pan or a double boiler. Cook over low heat or simmering water, stirring constantly until thickened. Add the butter, one piece at a time, stirring until incorporated before adding the next piece. Do not boil. When sauce is smooth and thick, season with salt, pepper and basil. Add okra and serve.

Yield: 4 servings

TOMATO CHEESE TART

1¼ cups onion and garlic
croutons
3 peeled and ¼-inch sliced
medium sized ripe
tomatoes
6 ounces grated mozzarella
cheese
4 sliced green onions
(include tops)

2 tablespoons dried basil
ground pepper to taste
4 tablespoons red wine
vinegar and oil salad
dressing
parsley or green onions
to garnish

In a 9-inch deep dish pie plate in alternating layers, place croutons, tomatoes, cheese, onions, basil and pepper. Top layer should be cheese. Microwave on high for 4 minutes. Remove from oven and spoon dressing over top. Let stand 5 minutes before serving. May be prepared ahead except for dressing, covered and refrigerated before baking. Allow to stand at room temperature 20 minutes before cooking. Garnish with fresh parsley or tops of green onions.

Yield: 4 to 6 servings

BAKED TOMATOES AND GREEN PEPPERS

8 tomatoes
2 green peppers, chopped
   finely
1 medium onion, chopped
   finely
2 tablespoons brown sugar
1 teaspoon salt
2 tablespoons butter

1 tablespoon all-purpose
   flour
   paprika
1 cup light cream
2 tablespoons chopped
   parsley to garnish
2 tablespoons chopped
   fresh basil to garnish

Cut tomatoes in half. Mix green peppers and onion with brown sugar and salt. Pat mixture on top of each tomato half, covering with as much as it will hold. Place in a baking dish in one layer, cover, and let stand at least 3 hours at room temperature. When ready to cook, pour off all juices which have accumulated in the bottom of the baking dish into a saucepan. Add the butter, flour and the paprika to the liquid and mix with a wire whisk. Add the cream. Bake the tomatoes in a 350° oven for 25 to 30 minutes. Allow the mixture in the saucepan to boil up once, then pour over the hot tomatoes. Garnish with parsley and basil.

Yield: 6 servings

TOMATO BASIL PIE

5   sliced medium tomatoes
1   9-inch pastry shell
½   cup mayonnaise
1   clove garlic, crushed
¼   teaspoon pepper

½   cup grated Parmesan
    cheese
½   cup fresh basil
6   soda crackers, crushed
2   teaspoons butter or
    margarine

Drain tomatoes on a paper towel, then place in the pastry shell. Mix mayonnaise, garlic, pepper, Parmesan cheese and basil. Spread over tomatoes. Sprinkle crushed crackers on top and dot with butter. Bake at 425° for 20 to 25 minutes. Let stand 10 to 15 minutes before cutting. Serve in pie-shaped wedges or can be cut in squares as an appetizer.

Yield: 6 to 8 servings

CREAMED SPINACH WITH ALLSPICE

3 pounds fresh spinach
½ cup butter
½ cup flour
1 cup half-and-half
1 teaspoon brown sugar
½ teaspoon allspice

½ teaspoon nutmeg
¼ teaspoon ground cloves
¼ teaspoon ground cinnamon
salt and pepper to taste
paprika to garnish

Wash and trim the spinach. Discard the stems. Either blanch the spinach in boiling water for 2 minutes or microwave, covered, for 1½ minutes. Drain it well, squeeze dry and chop it coarsely. (You may also use frozen chopped spinach, defrosted and squeezed dry.) In a large saucepan, melt the butter and stir in the flour. Cook the roux until bubbly for several minutes; add the half-and-half, stirring with a wire whisk to prevent lumps. Add brown sugar, allspice, nutmeg, cloves and cinnamon and continue stirring over low heat until the sauce is thick and smooth. Salt and pepper to taste. Combine with the spinach; simmer for a few minutes. Serve hot and garnish with the paprika.

Yield: 6 servings

GLAZED TURNIPS

3 tablespoons unsalted butter
1½ pounds white turnips, peeled and cut into 1-inch squares
1 cup chicken broth
1 teaspoon salt

¼ teaspoon freshly ground pepper
2 tablespoons sugar
2 tablespoons minced fresh parsley to garnish
2 tablespoons fresh sage to garnish

In a large skillet, melt the butter and toss the turnips to coat them. Add the broth, cover, and cook for 8 minutes. Increase the heat to high; season with salt and pepper and cook, uncovered, for about 10 minutes until the turnips are tender and the liquid is reduced and syrupy. Reduce the heat to moderate; sprinkle the turnips with the sugar and cook for about 1 minute until they are glazed and shiny. Garnish with the parsley and sage.

Yield: 4 to 6 servings

SWISS CHARD AND SPINACH

4 tablespoons virgin olive oil	1½ pounds Swiss chard, cooked and drained well
3 cloves garlic	½ teaspoon hot red pepper flakes
6 slices of bacon, cut in half	½ teaspoon coarse salt
3 tablespoons pine nuts	½ teaspoon freshly ground pepper
1½ pounds fresh spinach	

Heat the oil in a large skillet and cook bacon and garlic for 5 minutes, over a low flame and turning often. Discard the garlic and push the bacon to one side of the skillet. Add pine nuts and sauté for 2 minutes. Squeeze the greens dry, chop roughly and add to the skillet along with the pepper flakes, salt and pepper. Cook for 5 minutes, stirring occasionally. Empty the skillet onto a heated platter, arranging the bacon strips on top like spokes of a wheel. Serve hot.

Yield: 6 to 8 servings

ZUCCHINI FANS WITH SOUR CREAM SAUCE

8 small (4-inch long) zucchini	2 teaspoons tarragon vinegar
½ cup stock made with chicken stock concentrate	2 egg yolks
	½ teaspoon paprika
¾ cup sour cream	1 tablespoon fresh minced basil to garnish

Slice zucchini lengthwise almost to the end in many thin slices. Cook zucchini in a large skillet with chicken stock for about 3 minutes or just until bright green and slightly softened. Remove from the pan; drain on paper towels. Cook sour cream, vinegar, egg yolks and paprika in a heavy pan or double boiler, stirring constantly until thick and smooth. When ready to serve, arrange 2 zucchini fans on each plate, top with the sauce and salt lightly. Garnish with basil. Serve hot or at room temperature. If served hot, reheat the zucchini and sauce separately.

Yield: 4 servings

GRILLED VEGETABLE SANDWICHES

2 medium zucchini	4 submarine rolls or pita
2 baby white or purple	bread
eggplants	sliced tomatoes (optional)
2 large red onions	chopped black olives
2 tablespoons olive oil	(optional)
10 large basil leaves	fresh parsley to garnish

Clean zucchini, eggplant and onion. Slice zucchini lengthwise into ⅛-inch to ¼-inch thick slices. Do likewise with the onion and eggplant. Prepare grill. Lightly brush vegetables on both sides with olive oil. Grill zucchini 10 to 12 minutes turning several times; grill eggplant and onions 6 to 8 minutes turning several times. Arrange vegetables in layers on a flat plate, sprinkling remaining olive oil over them, interspersing the layers with basil leaves. Allow to sit at room temperature for a few hours for flavors to meld. If possible, use without refrigerating. If necessary to refrigerate allow vegetables to return to room temperature before making into sandwiches. Slice rolls or open pita bread. Fill with vegetables. Tomatoes and/or olives are a nice addition garnished with fresh parsley.

Yield: 4 servings

CITRUS COUSCOUS WITH BASIL AND APRICOTS

1 cup chicken stock	2 teaspoons orange zest
1 cup couscous	¼ cup chopped basil
1 teaspoon lemon zest	½ cup chopped dried
1 teaspoon lime zest	apricots

Bring stock and zests to a boil. Stir in couscous. Cover and remove from heat. Let stand 5 to 8 minutes. Stir in remaining ingredients.

Yield: 4 servings

BLUE CHEESE POLENTA

3 ounces blue cheese
2 cups milk
4 tablespoons butter
½ cup yellow cornmeal
  pinch of freshly grated
  nutmeg

⅛ teaspoon black pepper
¼ cup heavy cream
2 teaspoons salt
  strips of roasted red
  pepper or canned
  pimiento to garnish

Chop 1 ounce of the cheese and set aside. In a saucepan bring the milk and butter to a boil. Quickly add the cornmeal, stirring constantly with a wire whisk. Cook over medium heat, stirring constantly until the mixture becomes very thick. Add nutmeg, pepper and 1 ounce of chopped blue cheese, beating to keep the mixture smooth. Remove from heat; beat in the cream and salt. Heat oven to 400°. Butter or spray with vegetable spray 8 (⅓-cup) muffin tins and spoon in the cornmeal mixture. Let stand for 15 minutes until mixture cools and sets. Butter a heavy ovenproof baking pan and turn the cornmeal molds into it. Place a slice of the remaining blue cheese on top of each mold. Place in the oven for 15 minutes until the mounds begin to swell. Remove from oven and run under the broiler to glaze the tops. Use a broad spatula to transfer to serving plates. Garnish tops with several thin roasted red pepper strips or canned pimientos.

Yield: 8 servings

CREOLE RICE

3 cups water
1½ cups rice
6 tablespoons butter
  freshly ground black
  pepper
1 cup brine-cured pitted
  black olives

1 cup fresh chopped parsley
  leaves
2 large cloves garlic,
  pressed
¼ cup fresh thyme leaves
  or 1 teaspoon dried

Cook rice in boiling salted water, covered, until water is absorbed and rice is tender. Add remaining ingredients to rice. Stir until blended and serve.

Yield: 6 servings

CHINESE RIBBON RICE

4 tablespoons olive oil	1 green onion, minced including top
4 eggs	salt and pepper to taste
½ cup chopped black olives	2 to 4 cups cooked hot white rice
1 clove garlic, minced	

Warm oil over low heat in a large iron skillet. Beat eggs lightly. Mix in olives, garlic and onion. Season with salt and pepper to taste; pour into hot skillet, tipping to spread evenly. Turn off heat when barely solid and let cool in skillet. When cold, turn onto cutting board. Slice egg pancake into ½-inch ribbons. Mix ribbons into hot rice. Serve immediately or refrigerate and reheat. Delicious with pork.

Yield: 4 servings

CURRIED RICE WITH ALMONDS

1 cup uncooked white rice	1½ teaspoons curry powder
2 tablespoons vegetable oil	1 teaspoon salt
2 cups boiling water	¼ cup slivered almonds
1 medium onion, finely chopped	1 tablespoon butter

Cook and stir rice in oil until light brown. Pour rice into 1½-quart casserole. Stir in water, onion, curry and salt. Cover. Bake until rice is tender at 350° for about 30 minutes. Cook and stir almonds in butter until light brown. Stir into rice before serving.

Yield: 6 servings

RICE, SPINACH AND CHEESE BAKE

1   cup uncooked brown rice
2   cups cottage cheese
2   eggs
1   (10-ounce) package
    frozen chopped spinach,
    thawed and squeezed

1   (4-ounce) can chopped
    green chili or jalapeño
    peppers
6   ounces Monterey Jack
    cheese, cubed
1   teaspoon salt
    dash pepper
    grated nutmeg

Cook rice according to directions. Cut cheese into cubes. Combine all other ingredients, reserving some of the cubes of cheese. Stir into hot rice. Place in a 2-quart shallow baking dish. Dot with reserved cheese cubes. Bake at 350° for 30 minutes or until bubbly.

Yield: 4 to 6 servings

WILD RICE WITH ARTICHOKE CASSEROLE

1   cup uncooked wild rice
2¼   cups chicken broth
1½   cups fresh sliced
     mushrooms
1½   cups chopped celery
2   tablespoons butter
1   cup artichoke heart
     bottoms

¼   cup chopped scallions
3   tablespoons julienned
    carrots
2   tablespoons lemon juice
½   teaspoon thyme
    salt and pepper to taste

Simmer rice in chicken broth, covered, for 30 minutes. Sauté mushrooms and celery in butter. Add all other ingredients to skillet after heat is turned off. Combine all ingredients in a 2-quart casserole dish. Cover and bake in a 350° oven for 40 minutes.

Yield: 8 to 10 servings

WHITE OR RED BEANS WITH RICE

1	pound dried white or red beans	½	teaspoon white pepper
1½	pounds tasso, smoked sausage, pickled pork or ham hocks	1	teaspoon dried thyme
		½	teaspoon dried cumin
		½	teaspoon dried coriander
1	tablespoon chopped garlic	1	tablespoon dried basil
2	medium yellow onions, chopped	1	bay leaf
		2	cups chopped green onion
1	large bell pepper, chopped	1	cup chopped parsley
1	carrot, chopped	1	tablespoon Worcestershire sauce (optional)
2	teaspoons salt		
1	teaspoon black pepper	1	tablespoon Angostura bitters (optional)
½	teaspoon red pepper		

To pickle pork, marinate 1½ pounds cut into ½-inch cubes in cider vinegar for 3 days in a refrigerator. Discard marinade before adding meat to the bean mixture. Soak the beans overnight in water to cover. Cut whatever meat being used into ½-inch cubes or ½-inch slices. Place soaked drained beans in a large Dutch oven; add water to cover by about 2 inches. Bring to a boil and add everything except the green onions and parsley. Reduce heat to medium and let simmer, stirring occasionally, until the beans are tender. This will take anywhere from 1½ to 2½ hours. Check at 1½ hours to see if beans are tender; if mixture begins to dry out, add more water. When beans are tender, remove 2 to 3 cups and mash them against the side of the pot with a fork. This makes a thick gravy for the beans. Stir in the green onions and parsley. At this point, add Worcestershire and bitters if desired. Serve over rice.

Yield: 6 to 8 servings

BRAZILIAN BLACK BEANS AND RICE

Beans:

1¼	cups uncooked black beans		salt to taste
4	cups water	1	tablespoon oil
1	clove garlic, minced	1	cup chopped onion
1	small onion, peeled and stuck with 3 whole cloves	1	green pepper, chopped
		1½	cups uncooked rice

Salsa:

1	(16-ounce) can peeled tomatoes, drained	1	tablespoon wine vinegar
¾	cup diced red or white onion	1	teaspoon oil
2	cloves garlic, chopped	3	dashes hot pepper sauce or to taste
			fresh cilantro to garnish

To prepare beans, soak overnight. The next day, bring beans to a boil and then reduce heat to moderate. Cook for 1 hour. Add garlic and clove-studded onion. Salt to taste and cook for 1 hour longer. Beans should be tender but not mushy. Briefly sauté chopped onions and green peppers in oil. Remove whole onion with cloves from beans and discard. Add the sautéed onions and green peppers to the beans. Stir and cook a few minutes to blend flavors. Next, prepare rice according to package directions to make 4 cups.

To prepare salsa, in a small bowl break up tomatoes with a spoon. Mix in remaining ingredients, cover and refrigerate to let flavors blend. Serve black beans over cooked rice and top with salsa. Garnish with fresh cilantro.

Yield: 4 to 6 servings

POTATOES WITH ARUGULA SAUCE

24 small new red potatoes or 8 medium peeled russet potatoes
⅓ cup olive oil
3 cups arugula or watercress, including tender stems
½ cup chopped walnuts
2 tablespoons fresh thyme or 1 tablespoon dried

1½ teaspoons freshly ground pepper
⅓ cup olive oil
¾ cup whipping cream
1 tablespoon (or more) fresh lemon juice
½ cup chopped fresh mint leaves
1 teaspoon salt
mint sprigs for garnish

Cover potatoes with cold water in a large saucepan. Bring to a boil and cook until just tender. Drain. Cut new potatoes into ¼'s or russets into ⅛'s and place in large bowl. Add olive oil; mix to coat. Set aside. In a food processor, place arugula, walnuts, thyme and pepper. With machine running, gradually add oil, then cream. Mix in lemon juice. Pour sauce over the potatoes; add chopped mint and mix. Add salt and adjust lemon juice and salt if necessary. Serve potatoes at room temperature. Dish may be made 6 hours ahead and refrigerated, but bring to room temperature before serving.

Yield: 8 servings

ROAST POTATOES AND PARSNIPS

2 pounds peeled halved potatoes
2 pounds peeled halved parsnips

salt
8 tablespoons butter
¼ teaspoon paprika

Preheat oven to 375°. Cook the potatoes and parsnips in a large saucepan of lightly salted boiling water for 10 minutes. Drain. Put the butter in a baking dish, melt the butter in the oven and place parsnips and potatoes in the dish. Turn to coat all in butter. Roast for about 1 hour or until crunchy and golden. Sprinkle with paprika.

Yield: 6 to 8 servings

GRATIN OF POTATOES AND SPINACH

2	(10-ounce) packages frozen chopped spinach
2	pounds potatoes
1	cup minced onion
10	tablespoons butter
½	teaspoon sugar
	salt and pepper to taste

½	cup minced fresh parsley
½	cup freshly grated Parmesan or Romano cheese
4	tablespoons fresh bread crumbs

Thaw spinach, drain and squeeze dry. Scrub potatoes, slice in ⅛-inch thick slices crosswise and place in a bowl of cold water. In a large saucepan, cook the onion in 6 tablespoons of the butter, stirring for about 5 minutes or until soft. Add the spinach, sugar and salt and pepper. Cook over low heat for about 10 minutes. Stir in the parsley and ¼-cup cheese. Set aside. Bring salted water to a boil in a large saucepan. Drain the potato slices and place them in the salted water. Cook until just tender, about 5 minutes; drain. Run cold water over them to stop the cooking and pat the slices dry. Spray a 6-cup gratin dish with vegetable spray or butter it well. Arrange about ⅓ of the potato slices in the bottom. Spread the spinach mixture over the potatoes and arrange the remaining potato slices in a spiral pattern on top of the spinach. Sprinkle with the remaining ¼ cup cheese and the bread crumbs. Drizzle the remaining butter, melted, over all. Bake at 375° for about 30 minutes or until top is golden brown and dish is hot.

Yield: 4 to 6 servings

HERB POTATO CRISPS

1	Idaho baking potato per person

virgin olive oil
herb of choice

Preheat oven to 400°. Slice potatoes in ¼-inch rounds leaving skin on. Place on cookie sheets, which have been lightly greased with oil. Sprinkle potatoes with your favorite herbs such as basil, thyme, oregano or any combination. Bake for 15 to 18 minutes. Turn and bake another 15 minutes. Potatoes should be brown and crisp.

Yield: 1 potato per person

PARTY POTATOES

5 cups cooked cubed potatoes	1 cup sour cream
2 teaspoons salt	1 cup chopped green onions
2 cups small curd cottage cheese	1 cup shredded Cheddar cheese

Combine salt, cottage cheese, onions and sour cream. Fold into potatoes. Place in casserole and sprinkle with Cheddar cheese. Bake, covered, at 350° for 45 minutes.

Yield: 6 servings

TWICE BAKED SWEET POTATOES

6 medium sweet potatoes	1 tablespoon Beau Monde powder
3 tablespoons good blue cheese	1 teaspoon onion powder
¼ pound butter	1 teaspoon dried sage
¼ cup sour cream	1 tablespoon grated Romano cheese
½ teaspoon coarse black pepper	

Bake sweet potatoes until tender in either an oven or microwave. Cut ovals from the tops and scoop out potato and reserve the shells. With the potato, combine the remaining ingredients, except Romano cheese. Beat until very smooth. Return mixture to shells, mounding it. Sprinkle with cheese. Bake at 350° for 25 minutes or until puffed and lightly browned.

Yield: 6 servings

TOMATO CHUTNEY

4 pounds tomatoes, sliced
½ pound sugar
water
½ pound raisins
1 medium onion, chopped
3 ounces fresh ginger

1 lime, sliced and chopped
¼ teaspoon paprika
1 small hot chili
½ cup wine vinegar
1 tablespoon salt

Boil tomatoes with sugar and a little water. Add all the other ingredients and simmer until thick. Keep refrigerated. Wonderful with ham.

Yield: 6 cups

RHUBARB RELISH

1 quart rhubarb
1 quart chopped onions
4 cups brown sugar
½ teaspoon pepper
½ teaspoon ground cloves

1 teaspoon cinnamon
1 teaspoon salt
1 teaspoon allspice
2 cups white vinegar

Cut rhubarb into 1-inch pieces. Place all ingredients in a large saucepan. Bring to a boil, stirring occasionally. When thick, pour into sterilized jars and seal. Texture, appearance and flavor is much like green tomato relish.

Yield: 8 pints

CRANBERRY RELISH

2 cups washed raw cranberries
1 small onion

½ cup sugar
¾ cup sour cream
2 tablespoons horseradish

Mix all together in the blender. Freeze.

Yield: 6 servings

ARTICHOKE PICKLE

4 quarts diced Jerusalem
    artichokes
2 quarts chopped onions
6 red and green bell peppers
1 large head cauliflower,
    broken into flowerets

4 cups sugar
2 quarts vinegar
1 cup all-purpose flour
1 teaspoon turmeric
2 teaspoons dry mustard
¼ cup cold water

Soak vegetables overnight in brine (2 cups salt to 1 gallon water). Drain. Boil vinegar and sugar together. Make paste of flour, turmeric, dry mustard, and ¼ to ⅓ cup cold water. Add paste to boiling vinegar. Cook until entire mixture is thickened. Add all vegetables and simmer a few minutes. Seal in sterilized pint jars while still hot.

Yield: 16 pints

WATERMELON PICKLES

7 pounds watermelon rind
3½ pounds sugar
1 pint vinegar

½ teaspoon oil of cloves
½ teaspoon oil of cinnamon

Cut rind, outer skin removed, in approximately 1-inch lengths. Boil in salt water until tender; they will change color. Boil sugar, vinegar and spices to make a syrup. Pour over cooked rind. Stir well, cover, and leave on stove overnight. The next 2 mornings pour off syrup and bring to a boil. Pour back over pickles and stir well. Third morning, boil pickles and syrup together. Place in jars and seal.

Yield: 4 pints

PEPPER JELLY

¼ cup hot pepper sauce
1 cup finely chopped bell peppers
1½ cups vinegar

6 cups sugar
1 bottle Certo
green food coloring

Wear gloves to protect hands from pepper burns. Keep hands away from face. Cut peppers finely. Add sugar and vinegar and bring to a boil. Remove from heat. Skim. Add Certo, and food coloring if desired. Cool before sealing in hot sterilized jars.

Yield: 2 (6-ounce) jars

RED PEPPER SAUCE FOR PASTA

4 very red unblemished red peppers (about 1 pound)
1 to 2 peeled onions (about 1 pound)
¼ cup olive oil
1 tablespoon finely chopped garlic
½ teaspoon dried hot red pepper flakes

2 cups canned or fresh chicken broth
3 tablespoons tomato paste or purée
chopped sun-dried tomatoes
salt and freshly ground pepper to taste
¼ cup fresh chopped basil
Parmesan cheese

Cut the peppers in half. Cut away and discard the core, veins and seeds. Coarsely chop the peppers; there should be about 4 cups. Coarsely chop the onion; there should be about 4 cups. Heat the oil in a fairly deep skillet or casserole and add the peppers; cook, stirring about 5 minutes. Add the onions, garlic and red pepper flakes and cook, stirring often, about 2 minutes. Add the broth, tomatoes, salt and pepper; cover, and cook for about 15 minutes. Pour the mixture into the container of a food processor or electric blender and blend thoroughly. Pour the mixture into a saucepan and bring to a boil. Let cook about 2 minutes. Stir in the basil. Serve with pasta and grated Parmesan cheese on the side.

Yield: 4 servings

CARROT SAUCE FOR PASTA

¼ pound butter	6 tablespoons finely chopped carrot
3 tablespoons minced yellow onion	2½ cups canned Italian tomatoes with juice
3 tablespoons finely chopped celery	½ cup heavy cream (optional)

Place all ingredients in a heavy saucepan. Simmer for 1 hour, stirring occasionally with a wooden spoon. Purée contents in a blender or food processor until very smooth. Serve over favorite pasta. If you wish to make a richer sauce, add ½ cup heavy cream after you purée. Reheat to simmer. Serve.

Yield: 4 to 6 servings

WALNUT SAUCE FOR PASTA

1 cup freshly shelled walnuts	¼ cup fresh basil
3 heaping tablespoons pine nuts	¾ cup olive oil
	freshly grated nutmeg to taste
1 to 2 large peeled cloves garlic	salt to taste
	½ pound pasta of choice

Blanch walnuts in boiling water for 3 minutes; dry with paper towels and rub off skins. Arrange pine nuts in a single layer in a pie plate. Roast at 350° about 10 minutes or until golden. Watch carefully so they don't get too brown. Finely mince garlic and basil together. Put ¼ cup olive oil in a skillet; add garlic mixture to pan. Transfer walnuts and pine nuts to blender or food processor container; blend until a thick paste results. Spoon this paste into the skillet and mix well with garlic mixture. If it is too dry to toss with pasta, stir in some extra olive oil. Sauce should be slightly thick. Cook slowly over low heat, about 5 minutes, stirring often to prevent burning. Check consistency again. If too thick, add additional olive oil and some boiling water. Add nutmeg and salt to taste; stir well. Cook pasta of choice according to package directions; drain. Toss with walnut sauce and transfer to serving platter. Serve immediately.

Yield: 4 servings

SAUSAGE SAUCE PIQUANT

1 tablespoon all-purpose
  flour
1 tablespoon olive oil
1 pound smoked sausage,
  diced
2 small onions, chopped

½ bell pepper, chopped
1 (28-ounce) can tomatoes
¼ cup water
  salt, pepper and red
  pepper to taste

Combine flour and oil in a heavy skillet. Stir constantly until it turns a dark chocolate brown. Be very careful not to burn. Add diced sausage, onion and bell pepper. Cook until vegetables are soft. Add tomatoes, ¼ cup water, salt, pepper and red pepper. Cover and simmer about 1 hour. Serve over rice.

Yield: 4 servings

PISTACHIO PESTO

¼ pound unrinsed basil
  leaves (6 cups loosely
  packed)
½ cup shelled unsalted
  pistachios
1 cup loosely packed
  parsley

½ cup grated Romano
  cheese
  salt and freshly ground
  pepper to taste
3 to 4 tablespoons finely
  chopped garlic
¾ to 1 cup olive oil

Rinse basil carefully and pat or spin dry. Set aside. If pistachios have not been blanched, bring enough water to boil to cover pistachios when added. Add pistachios; simmer about 2 minutes or until the outer coating can be removed easily with fingers. Drain; remove outer coating; set aside. Put basil into food processor; add pistachios, parsley, cheese, salt, pepper and garlic. Start processing and gradually add oil in a fine stream. Process until almost totally smooth in texture. The sauce should be thinned with a little water in which your pasta is cooking. This sauce freezes well.

Yield: 2½ cups

PESTO SAUCE

2 cups loosely packed fresh basil leaves
5 sprigs of parsley
1 teaspoon coarse salt
3 medium cloves garlic, cut in half
2 tablespoons toasted pine nuts

2 tablespoons toasted chopped walnuts
1 tablespoon grated Romano cheese
1 tablespoon grated Parmesan cheese
½ to ¾ cup olive oil

Blend dry ingredients in a food processor using on/off switch quickly. Then slowly add olive oil. Scrape and stop when thick. Don't heat. Serve over hot pasta. Can be frozen, but leave cheeses out and add them after pesto has reached room temperature.

Yield: 1½ cups

TOMATO SAUCE FOR SPAGHETTI OR PIZZA

1 (46-ounce) can tomato juice
1 (28-ounce) can tomato purée or Italian plum tomatoes
2 (6-ounce) cans tomato sauce
1 (6-ounce) can tomato paste
2 cloves garlic, finely minced or pressed
3 onions, finely chopped

3 tablespoons beef stock or 3 bouillon cubes
1½ tablespoons chili powder
1 tablespoon basil
1 tablespoon oregano
2 teaspoons salt
½ teaspoon ground pepper
1 tablespoon sugar
1 tablespoon margarine
3 pounds ground sirloin (optional)
1 pound ground pork (optional)

Place all ingredients in a large stock pot and simmer for at least 4 hours. If using ground sirloin and/or pork, sauté until no longer pink and add to sauce while simmering. If possible, let finished sauce sit overnight in the refrigerator since it will become more flavorful if it is allowed to sit and marinate. Use for topping pastas or pizza.

Yield: 12 cups

MUSTARD DILL SAUCE

⅓ cup Dijon mustard
½ cup sour cream
   juice of 1 lemon
1 clove garlic, crushed

½ cup chopped fresh dill or
   1 teaspoon dried
   pinch of cayenne pepper

Mix all ingredients together in medium bowl. Use as a spread on fish steaks, fillets or chicken breasts wrapped in foil and broiled or grilled. Serve as a sauce with grilled fish or chicken.

Yield: 1⅓ cups

MUSTARD AND HONEY SAUCE FOR FISH

2 tablespoons grated onion
2 tablespoons butter
2 tablespoons all-purpose
   flour

1 cup champagne or dry
   white vermouth
1 teaspoon Dijon mustard
1 teaspoon honey
¼ teaspoon salt

Sauté onion in the butter until limp. Stir in the flour and cook until bubbly and flour is cooked through. With a wire whisk, beat in the wine and cook stirring constantly until smooth and thick. Remove from heat. Add mustard, honey and salt. Taste and adjust seasoning as desired. Sauce may be put through the blender or food processor if desired. This is particularly desirable if a larger quantity is made.

Yield: 1½ cups

MUSTARD MARINADE

¼ cup Dijon mustard
½ cup white wine vinegar
1 to 2 cloves garlic, mashed

2 tablespoons minced onion
½ teaspoon crushed
   rosemary

Combine all ingredients. Use as marinade for whole chicken pieces skinned or skin-on. Grill or broil. Chicken is good hot or cold, great as left-overs sliced for sandwiches or placed on greens for salad. Marinade could also be used for fish, beef or pork.

Yield: 1 cup

CARIBBEAN MARINADE FOR PORK OR CHICKEN

1 clove garlic, finely minced or ½ teaspoon prepared minced garlic
1 tablespoon ground ginger
1 teaspoon salt
1 teaspoon allspice
¼ teaspoon black pepper
1 bay leaf, crumbled

¼ cup dark rum
⅔ cup firmly packed brown sugar
1 tablespoon fresh lime juice
1 tablespoon grated lime peel

Mix all ingredients together. To use with pork, pour over and rub into a 3½ pound boneless or a 5 pound bone-in pork loin. Cover with plastic wrap and marinate for at least 2 hours or overnight in the refrigerator. To use with chicken, pour over chicken and cover dish with plastic wrap. Marinate for 2 to 4 hours.

Yield: Enough for 3 to 5 pounds of meat

BOURBON MARINADE FOR PORK

¼ cup bourbon
¼ cup soy sauce
¼ cup Dijon mustard
¼ cup minced scallions
¼ cup brown sugar

1 teaspoon salt
1 teaspoon Worcestershire sauce
freshly ground pepper to taste

Combine all ingredients in a dish. Marinate pork overnight in the refrigerator.

Yield: 1¼ cups

MOP SAUCE FOR MEAT OR POULTRY

1 cup cider vinegar
5 tablespoons
   Worcestershire sauce
⅔ cup salad oil
3 tablespoons butter
1 lemon, thinly sliced
3 cloves garlic, minced

3 tablespoons fresh
   chopped ginger
2 tablespoons dry mustard
½ teaspoon dried thyme
1 cup brown sugar
   (optional)
½ cup ketchup (optional)

Put all ingredients into a food processor or blender and run until smooth. Pour into a saucepan and heat for about 20 minutes to blend the flavors. A barbecue sauce may be made by adding the brown sugar and ketchup. Use mop sauce to baste any meat or poultry while cooking. Add barbecue sauce after cooking or meat will be blackened.

Yield: 2 to 3 cups

HORSERADISH SAUCE

3 tablespoons grated fresh
   horseradish or well-
   drained prepared bottled
   horseradish
1 teaspoon salt
½ teaspoon dry mustard
½ teaspoon powdered sugar

1 tablespoon heavy cream
¾ cup whipped heavy cream
2 tablespoons malt vinegar
   or lemon juice
⅛ teaspoon hot pepper
   sauce
4 teaspoons ground walnuts

In a small bowl work together the horseradish, salt, dry mustard and sugar. Add the cream to make a smooth paste. Fold the mixture into the whipped cream. Mix in the vinegar or lemon juice, hot pepper sauce and fold in nuts. Serve at room temperature. Serve with cold roast beef or pork, corned beef, smoked trout or vegetables.

Yield: 1 cup

MOLE SAUCE

1   corn tortilla
1   to 2 tablespoons chili
    powder
½   teaspoon cinnamon
½   teaspoon ground cloves
½   teaspoon ground
    coriander
½   teaspoon fresh chopped
    cilantro
5   tablespoons almonds
1   onion, chopped

2   cloves garlic, chopped
3   tomatoes, peeled, seeded
    and chopped
1½ cups raisins
2   tablespoons sesame seeds
¼   teaspoon salt
4   tablespoons vegetable oil
2   cups chicken broth
1½ ounces semi-sweet
    chocolate

Tear tortilla into small pieces. In a large bowl, blend all except last 3 ingredients. In a separate pan, heat vegetable oil, chicken broth and chocolate. Add ingredients from large bowl into saucepan, stirring over low heat with whisk until chocolate is completely melted. Liquid should be the consistency of heavy cream. Allow mixture to cool. Will keep in a refrigerator for a week. To use, reheat and spoon over freshly cooked turkey or chicken.

Yield: 2 to 3 cups

BARBECUE SAUCE

¼   cup salad oil
¾   cup chopped onions
1   clove garlic, chopped
1   cup honey
1   cup ketchup
1   cup wine vinegar

½   cup Worcestershire sauce
1½ tablespoons dry mustard
1½ teaspoons salt
1   teaspoon pepper
1   teaspoon dried oregano
½   teaspoon dried thyme

Cook garlic and onions in salad oil until tender. Add remaining ingredients and cook until boiling, stirring constantly. Simmer 15 minutes.

Yield: 3 to 3½ cups

ARTICHOKES IN ROQUEFORT DRESSING

¼ pound butter
1 wedge Roquefort cheese
  lemon to taste

1 (8.5-ounce) can artichoke
  hearts

In a double boiler, melt the butter and add the cheese and lemon juice. Drain the artichoke hearts and add to the sauce. Heat over low flame for 15 to 20 minutes. Serve hot as an accompaniment to steak.

Yield: 2 to 4 servings

ENGLISH APPLESAUCE FOR PORK OR CHICKEN

3 large cooking apples,
  sliced
1 shallot, chopped
1 tablespoon sugar

1 tablespoon butter
1 tablespoon sherry
1 teaspoon vanilla
  salt and pepper to taste

Cook all ingredients very gently. Do not add water. Stir occasionally. Mixture is done when it is thick and chunky. Store in refrigerator.

Yield: 1 cup

SALADS
and
DRESSINGS

The fire destroyed the St. James Cathedral,
Chicago's first Episcopal Church. All that
remained standing was the belltower.

SALADS

DRESSINGS

CHICKEN SALAD WITH CAPERS AND PECANS

2 whole chicken breasts
1 (4-ounce) jar capers, drained
2 cups dry vermouth or chicken stock

½ cup chopped green onion
¾ cup pecans
mayonnaise
Dijon mustard
lemon juice

Poach chicken breasts in dry vermouth or chicken stock. Cool and cut into cubes. Toss chicken, capers, green onions and pecans together. Combine mayonnaise, Dijon mustard and lemon juice in a small bowl. Add to the chicken mixture and toss to coat the ingredients. Serve on a bed of lettuce.

Yield: 2 servings

CHICKEN CAESAR SALAD

2 whole chicken breasts, skinned and boned
½ cup white Worcestershire sauce
1 teaspoon anchovy paste
2 cloves garlic, pressed
2 tablespoons lemon juice

1 tablespoon Dijon mustard
⅓ cup olive oil
1 head Romaine lettuce, washed and torn
4 tablespoons grated Parmesan cheese
seasoned croutons

Marinate the chicken in Worcestershire sauce for several hours. Cover with foil and bake 30 minutes in a 350° oven. Cool and cut into bite-sized chunks. Combine anchovy paste, garlic, lemon juice and mustard. Whisk until smooth. Slowly whisk in the olive oil. Add chicken to lettuce. Toss with the dressing. Add croutons and sprinkle with Parmesan cheese.

Yield: 6 to 8 servings

HOT CHICKEN SALAD

2 whole chicken breasts, skinned and boned
3 cups chicken stock
4 cups chopped celery
2 teaspoons salt
½ teaspoon tarragon
⅓ cup grated onion
1 tablespoon lemon juice
2 cups mayonnaise
¼ cup dry vermouth
1 cup sliced toasted almonds
1 cup bread crumbs or crushed corn flakes
½ cup grated Parmesan or Romano cheese

Poach the chicken breasts in the chicken stock. Cool and cut into cubes. Combine chicken, celery, salt, tarragon, onion, lemon juice, mayonnaise, vermouth and toasted almonds. Refrigerate at least 1 hour. Spoon into a buttered 11 x 7 x 2-inch baking dish. Cover the top with bread crumbs and grated cheese. Bake 30 minutes at 350° or until hot.

Yield: 6 to 8 servings

WARM CHICKEN, BEAN, RICE AND CORN SALAD

½ cup rice
1 cup water
2 whole chicken breasts, boned and skinned
2 tablespoons olive oil
2 tablespoons fresh lime juice
2 tablespoons red wine vinegar
1 tablespoon ground cumin
3 scallions, thinly sliced
1 jalapeño chili, stemmed, seeded and minced
1 clove garlic, minced
1 (15-ounce) can kidney beans, rinsed well and drained
1 (13-ounce) can corn avocado (optional)

Combine rice with water and bring to a boil. Reduce heat to simmer and cover. Cook a total of 17 minutes until liquid is absorbed and rice is tender. Grill or broil chicken breasts about 10 minutes or until done. In a serving bowl, beat olive oil, lime juice and vinegar; add cumin. Stir in scallions, jalapeño and garlic. Cut chicken into bite-sized pieces and add with beans to dressing. About 5 minutes before rice is done, stir in corn to heat. Stir rice mixture into dressing. If using avocado, cut up directly into bowl and stir gently.

Yield: 6 to 8 servings

WARM SALAD OF HAM, RASPBERRIES AND ONIONS

4 ounces tiny white pearl onions	16 small spinach leaves, washed and dried
2 cups dry red wine	1 cup raspberries
⅔ cup orange juice	¼ teaspoon coarse pepper
¼ cup sugar	1 tablespoon finely chopped fresh basil or ½ teaspoon dried
1 navel orange	
12 ounces good smoked ham, sliced ¼-inch thick	

Cut the root ends off the onions. In a large pot of boiling water, blanch the onions for 2 minutes. Drain and when cool enough slip off the skins. Reserve onions. In a large skillet, combine the wine, orange juice and sugar. Bring to a boil and stir to dissolve the sugar. Cook for 6 minutes. Add the onions and cook for another 6 minutes. The onions should be tender and the liquid reduced to almost ½ cup of syrup; reserve. Remove a large piece of zest from the orange with a vegetable peeler and cut it into very fine slivers. Blanch for 30 seconds in boiling water. Pour cold water over it and reserve on paper towels. Using a sharp knife, remove the remaining peel and white pith from the orange. Section the orange and allow to sit in a strainer to drain off any juice. Trim the ham of any fat, and cut into strips. Arrange the spinach leaves in circles on 2 plates. Add the ham to the onions and wine sauce. Heat for 1 minute and stir to coat the ham. Add the orange sections, berries and pepper and toss to coat. Using a slotted spoon, divide the salad mixture between the spinach-lined plates. Pour remaining sauce over it and garnish with the orange zest. Serve warm.

Yield: 2 servings

WARM APPLE AND GOAT CHEESE SALAD

1 small clove garlic
2 tablespoons red wine vinegar
½ teaspoon Dijon mustard
½ teaspoon salt
½ teaspoon pepper
⅓ cup olive oil

1 tablespoon chopped fresh parsley
3 Belgian endives
1 bunch watercress
1 Granny Smith apple
1½ ounces log-shaped goat cheese
¼ cup chopped walnuts

Mince garlic. Shake vinegar, mustard, salt and pepper in small jar. Add oil and parsley; shake again. Heat broiler. Arrange endive leaves like spokes on a plate. Put watercress in the center. Core and slice the apple. Arrange the slices slightly overlapping in 4 fans on baking pan. Cut the cheese into 4 slices and top each fan of apples with a round of cheese. Broil until golden, about 5 minutes. With spatula, put apples and cheese on top of endive. Pour dressing over salads and sprinkle with nuts. Serve at once.

Yield: 4 servings

SPINACH SALAD WITH STRAWBERRIES

Salad:
10 ounces fresh spinach, washed and dried

1 pound fresh strawberries, hulled and halved, if large

Lemon dressing:
¼ cup sugar
juice of 1 large lemon (3 tablespoons)

6 tablespoons vegetable oil

To make the salad, stem and tear spinach into bite-size pieces. Place in a bowl with the strawberries and chill well.

To make the dressing, dissolve the sugar in the lemon juice in a medium bowl. With a wire whisk, beat the oil in slowly until the dressing is emulsified. Cover and refrigerate. At serving time, whisk again, if necessary. Pour over salad and toss.

Yield: 6 servings

TOMATOES AND FIELD GREENS

12 ripe tomatoes, thickly sliced
¼ cup chopped green onions
½ cup olive oil
⅓ cup wine vinegar
8 basil leaves or 2 teaspoons dried
1 teaspoon salt
½ teaspoon dry mustard
2 cloves garlic, crushed
1 tablespoon minced parsley
1 teaspoon sugar
1 cup coarsely grated mozzarella cheese
assorted field greens
chopped parsley and sweet onion rings to garnish

Slice tomatoes. Combine all remaining ingredients except greens and mozzarella in a bowl and pour over tomatoes. Marinate 4 to 8 hours. Place on bed of field greens. Cover with grated mozzarella cheese. Garnish with chopped parsley and sweet onion rings.

Yield: 12 servings

BIBB AND RADICCHIO SALAD

2 tablespoons balsamic vinegar
4 tablespoons virgin olive oil
2 heads Bibb or Boston lettuce
1 small head radicchio
1 log Chevre cheese
1 cup fresh bread crumbs
½ cup chopped walnuts

Mix vinegar and oil and set aside. Wash and dry lettuce and radicchio. On each plate lay 4 lettuce leaves to form a flat bowl. Shred remaining lettuce and radicchio and distribute in the center of 4 plates. Cut cheese log into 6 rounds. Dip cheese into bread crumbs. Place cheese on a piece of wax paper on microwavable plate. Microwave for 45 seconds at 70% power. Continue to microwave at 15 second intervals until cheese is soft and warm, but not runny. Drizzle vinaigrette over greens. Add one warm cheese round in the center of each plate. Sprinkle walnuts on greens. Serve.

Yield: 6 servings

BLUE CHEESE AND ROMAINE SALAD

1 clove garlic
1 cup olive oil
1 cup blue cheese (best grade)
1 large head Romaine lettuce, torn into pieces
1 cup croutons
freshly ground black pepper
¼ cup freshly grated Parmesan cheese
1 tablespoon lemon juice

With the back of a spoon, crush the garlic in a wooden bowl until it disappears into the wood. Add the olive oil, then crush the cheese into the oil until it resembles cream. Add the lettuce, toss well. Sprinkle with croutons, black pepper and cheese. Sprinkle with lemon juice and serve.

Yield: 4 servings

CURRIED COLESLAW

2 cups finely shredded cabbage
1 green onion, finely minced
1 (10-ounce) package early frozen peas, thawed
¼ cup sour cream
¼ cup mayonnaise
¼ teaspoon curry powder
¼ teaspoon salt
dash of pepper
1 teaspoon prepared mustard
1 teaspoon wine vinegar
¾ cup chopped salted peanuts to garnish

In a salad bowl, mix together cabbage, onion and peas. In a small bowl, mix remaining ingredients except peanuts. Pour dressing over chopped cabbage mixture, tossing lightly. Cover and refrigerate for at least 1 hour or overnight. Garnish with peanuts before serving.

Yield: 8 servings

CRUNCHY CABBAGE SALAD

Salad:
- 1 head green cabbage
- 1 package Oriental chicken-flavored noodle mix (reserve chicken flavor packet for dressing)
- 4 green onions, sliced thinly

Dressing:
- ½ cup salad oil
- 1 tablespoon sugar
- ½ teaspoon black pepper
- 1 package chicken flavoring from noodle mix
- 2 tablespoons toasted sesame seeds
- ½ cup sliced toasted almonds

Shred or finely chop cabbage. Add onions and crushed dry noodles. Mix well and cover; set in refrigerator for 1 hour. Mix dressing ingredients thoroughly. Refrigerate until serving time. Toast seeds and almonds in 350° oven for 7 minutes. Toss dressing with cabbage mixture. Add seeds and almonds.

Yield: 10 servings

SAUERKRAUT SALAD

- ½ cup white or cider vinegar
- 1½ cups sugar
- 2 (16-ounce) cans sauerkraut, drained
- 1 small jar pimientos, finely chopped
- ½ green pepper, chopped
- ½ cup chopped green onion (no green tops)
- ½ cup chopped celery

Heat sugar and vinegar to boiling point. Allow to cool. Mix all of the remaining ingredients in a large bowl. Add cooled dressing and mix well. Refrigerate in a ½ gallon container for at least 48 hours before serving. Keeps for several weeks in refrigerator.

Yield: 6 servings

PEA, SWEET ONION AND MINT SALAD

1 (16-ounce) bag frozen
   green peas
2 tablespoons salad oil
3 tablespoons minced fresh
   mint (do not use dried)

2 teaspoons salt
2 teaspoons honey
1 medium red onion, sliced
   very thin into rounds for
   decoration

Dressing:
⅓ cup sour cream

1½ tablespoons white wine
   vinegar

Boil the frozen peas no longer than 5 minutes (crisp-tender). Cool immediately under cold water to stop cooking. Combine oil, mint, salt and honey and mix with the peas. Refrigerate for 4 hours or overnight. Combine the peas, onions and dressing and serve.

Yield: 4 servings

PEA AND BACON SALAD

Salad:
1 (20-ounce) bag frozen
   peas
8 slices cooked crisp bacon,
   crumbled

¼ cup chopped green onions
2 tablespoons chopped
   parsley
   salt and pepper to taste

Dressing:
¼ cup sour cream
¼ cup mayonnaise

1 large tablespoon Dijon
   mustard

Rinse peas under hot water until defrosted; drain well. Put paper towels under peas in a bowl and refrigerate. Mix dressing ingredients. Remove paper towels from bowl and combine peas with all the ingredients and dressing. Salt and pepper to taste. Serve chilled.

Yield: 6 to 8 servings

MINTED POTATO AND PEA SALAD

1½ pounds boiling potatoes,
quartered lengthwise and
cut crosswise into ¾-inch
slices
2 tablespoons vinegar
salt and pepper to taste
½ cup mayonnaise
3 tablespoons minced fresh
mint leaves or 1
tablespoon dried

1 cup cooked fresh peas
(about 1-pound
unshelled) or thawed
frozen peas
½ cup chopped onion
1 to 2 tablespoons water
(optional)

In a steamer set over boiling water, steam the potatoes, covered, for 8 to 10 minutes or until they are just tender. Transfer them to a bowl and toss them with 1 tablespoon of the vinegar and salt to taste. Let the potatoes cool and chill them, covered, for 1 hour or until they are cold. In a second bowl, thin the mayonnaise with the remaining tablespoon of vinegar and stir in the mint. Pour the dressing over the potatoes. Add the peas and onion, salt and pepper to taste and toss the potato salad. If desired, thin the potato salad with 1 to 2 tablespoons of water.

Yield: 4 servings

WHITE BEAN AND POTATO SALAD

6 medium boiling potatoes
2 tablespoons finely
chopped onion
1 cup cooked white beans
such as Great Northern
½ cup mayonnaise
½ cup sour cream

½ cup cooked beets, cut into
¼-inch cubes (either
fresh, canned or drained)
salt and pepper
fresh chopped parsley to
garnish

Boil potatoes until just cooked but not falling apart. Cool slightly and peel. Place in a large bowl, add onion and cooked beans. Combine mayonnaise and sour cream and add to potato mixture, being careful not to crush beans or potatoes. Add salt and pepper to taste. May be made one day ahead. Just before serving, carefully stir in beet cubes. Garnish with freshly chopped parsley.

Yield: 6 to 8 servings

THAI BLACK BEAN SALAD

1   (16-ounce) can black
   beans
½   cup onion
½   cup red pepper
½   cup celery
¼   cup cilantro
1   cup canned corn
1   teaspoon minced ginger
   root

3   tablespoons sesame oil
2   tablespoons rice (or
   white) vinegar
1   tablespoon lime juice
1   clove
1   lime, cut into wedges to
   garnish
1   tomato, sliced to garnish
   salt to taste

Rinse and drain beans. Chop onion, pepper, celery and cilantro. Combine all solid ingredients in a large bowl. Whisk liquids together in a small bowl, adding salt to taste. Pour over solid ingredients and chill for 1 hour. Serve on a bed of lettuce and garnish with wedges of lime and tomatoes. May be prepared ahead up to one day in advance.

Yield: 4 servings

SOUTHWESTERN CORN SALAD

1   cup dried black beans
1   pound package frozen
   corn
9   ounce package frozen
   white corn
1   large red pepper, diced
4   green onions, thinly sliced

¼   cup minced fresh cilantro,
   or more to taste
1   cup fresh lime juice
¼   teaspoon salt
⅛   teaspoon coarsely ground
   black pepper

Cook black beans according to package directions; drain and cool to room temperature. Defrost corn but do not cook. Combine all ingredients and refrigerate for at least 1 hour. Mix prior to serving and drain excess liquid. Mound on lettuce-lined platter or bowl.

Yield: 4 to 6 servings

RICE SALAD

4½ tablespoons butter
3 tablespoons chopped onion
3 cups rice
4 cups water
3 teaspoons salt
2 cups chicken broth
10 radishes

1 green pepper
½ onion
12 mint leaves
4½ ounces chopped black olives
2 tablespoons olive oil
2 teaspoons vinegar

Melt 1 tablespoon butter, stir in onion and sauté. Add rice and stir for 2 minutes. Add water, 3½ tablespoons butter, salt, broth and stir while bringing to a boil. Lower the heat, cover and simmer for 20 minutes. Remove cover, pour rice into large bowl and fluff with a fork. Chop radishes, green pepper, onion, mint leaves and olives; add to rice; cool to room temperature. Add oil and vinegar; toss. Refrigerate overnight.

Yield: 8 servings

CURRY RICE SALAD

1½ cups rice
1 chicken bouillon cube
3⅓ cups water
4 to 6 green onions, chopped
¼ cup chopped green peppers
¼ cup chopped red peppers
12 to 16 pimiento olives, cut small

2 (6-ounce) jars marinated artichoke hearts, cut into pieces
¾ to 1 teaspoon curry powder
½ cup mayonnaise
1 (6-ounce) jar artichoke marinade juice

Cook rice in water to which bouillon cube has been added. Combine cooked rice with all other ingredients and chill several hours before serving.

Yield: 6 servings

SPICY SESAME NOODLE SALAD

Dressing:

2 tablespoons red wine vinegar

2 tablespoons soy sauce

2 tablespoons smooth peanut butter

1 tablespoon minced fresh ginger root

2 cloves garlic, minced

2 teaspoons sugar

4 tablespoons olive oil

2 tablespoons sesame oil

Salad:

12 ounces whole wheat or regular vermicelli

4 ounces snow peas

4 ounces smoked ham

1 bunch (approximately 1 cup) scallions

coarsely ground black pepper to taste

½ teaspoon red pepper flakes to garnish

Make dressing by whisking the first 6 ingredients together in a bowl. In a separate small bowl, whisk the oils. Then whisk the oils into the first bowl of ingredients. Break pasta into 4-inch lengths and cook in boiling water for 5 to 6 minutes. Cut peas in half diagonally. Cut the ham into thin strips. Thinly slice the scallions. Toss the snow peas into the boiling pasta water and cook for 30 seconds. Drain pasta and peas under cold water and allow to dry. Mix the salad ingredients. Toss with the dressing. Chill before serving, 15 minutes up to 8 hours. Serve and garnish with red pepper flakes.

Yield: 4 servings

TORTELLINI SALAD

¼ cup olive oil
2 tablespoons white wine vinegar
¼ cup chopped green onion
2 cloves garlic
1 tablespoon crumbled dried basil
1 teaspoon dried dill

2 (12-ounce) packages frozen tortellini
1 (8½-ounce) can water-packed artichoke hearts, drained and quartered
1 large tomato, chopped
½ cup crumbled Feta cheese
½ cup chopped black olives
½ cup chopped walnuts

Whisk oil and vinegar in a small bowl. Add onion, garlic, basil and dill and mix well. Cook the tortellini according to package instructions. Combine tortellini and the remaining ingredients into a large bowl. Pour dressing over it and toss gently. Refrigerate overnight before serving.

Yield: 6 servings as a main course; 12 servings as a side dish

POMEGRANATE FRUIT SALAD

Salad:
2 grapefruits
1 large apple

¼ cup pomegranate seeds
5 to 10 whole lettuce leaves

Dressing:
1 (3-ounce) package cream cheese
¼ cup mayonnaise
¼ cup pineapple juice

2 tablespoons honey
½ teaspoon celery seed
¼ teaspoon salt

To make salad, peel, section and remove membrane from grapefruit sections. Slice apple; arrange fruit on lettuce leaves. Top with dressing and sprinkle pomegranate seeds over dressing. Oranges or pears may be substituted for grapefruit and apple.

To make dressing, soften cream cheese to room temperature. Blend in mayonnaise until smooth. Gradually add pineapple juice and honey, blending until smooth. Add celery seed and salt.

Yield: 4 servings

PEAR SALAD WITH RASPBERRY VINAIGRETTE

1 cup frozen red
  raspberries
¼ cup red wine vinegar
¼ cup salad oil
1 tablespoon sugar
¼ teaspoon ground
  cinnamon

4 cups torn mixed salad
  greens
2 cored and sliced pears
1 cup halved red grapes
¼ cup chopped pecans

Thaw raspberries. In blender or food processor, combine raspberries and vinegar. Cover and blend or process until berries are pureed. Strain mixture and discard seeds; stir in salad oil, sugar and cinnamon; cover and chill. Arrange salad greens on 4 plates. Top with pear slices. Top pears with halved grapes and sprinkle with pecans. Drizzle dressing over each salad.

Yield: 4 servings

GRAPEFRUIT, CRANBERRY AND BANANA SALAD

3 medium grapefruits,
  sectioned
1 cup grapefruit juice
1 cup sugar

½ cup orange marmalade
2 cups fresh or frozen
  cranberries
2 bananas

Section grapefruit and save juice. Add water to juice to make 1 cup. Mix juice with sugar and orange marmalade. Bring to a boil and stir well. Add cranberries. Cook until cranberries are all popped, about 2 to 10 minutes. Let cool; add grapefruit. Stir and chill. Just before serving add 2 sliced bananas.

Yield: 6 servings

BANANA SALAD

1 beaten egg	1 tablespoon butter
1 cup sugar	6 firm bananas
3 tablespoons water	dry roasted salted
1½ tablespoons cider vinegar	chopped peanuts

Combine egg, sugar, water, vinegar and butter in a small, heavy saucepan. Cook over medium heat until boiling; remove. Cut bananas lengthwise and place in a serving bowl. Layer bananas, sauce and peanuts. Serve at room temperature. Great for picnics.

Yield: 6 servings

BALSAMIC VINEGAR DRESSING

2 cloves garlic, minced	2 twists fresh pepper
2 tablespoons Dijon mustard	½ cup olive oil
1 tablespoon dried dill	¼ cup balsamic vinegar

Mix the first 4 ingredients; let sit for 15 minutes. Add the oil and vinegar; mix well.

Yield: 1 cup

CELERY SEED DRESSING

⅔ cup sugar	⅓ cup white vinegar
1 teaspoon dry mustard	⅓ cup honey
1 teaspoon paprika	¼ cup water
¼ teaspoon salt	½ cup salad oil
1 teaspoon celery seed	

Combine all ingredients except oil. Blend on low speed with a hand mixer in a small bowl until smooth. Gradually add oil, continuing to blend on medium speed until thick.

Yield: 1½ cups

CURRY DRESSING

3 shallots, minced
3 tablespoons Dijon
  mustard
4 tablespoons fresh lime
  juice
1 egg yolk or ½ cup egg
  substitute

1 tablespoon curry powder
⅓ cup olive oil
⅓ cup safflower oil
¼ cup sour cream
1 tablespoon chopped
  chives

Whisk together shallots, mustard, lime juice, egg yolk and curry powder. Whisk in oil until mixture is thick. Fold in sour cream and chives.

Yield: 1½ cups

HONEY FRENCH DRESSING

⅔ cup cider vinegar
½ cup sugar
2 teaspoons salt
2 teaspoons dry mustard
1 teaspoon paprika

½ tablespoon cornstarch
3 tablespoons water
¼ cup honey
1 cup vegetable oil
¼ small onion wedge

In container, shake together vinegar, sugar, salt, mustard and paprika. Dissolve cornstarch in water; add to jar and shake again. Add honey, shake. Add oil, shake. Float wedge of onion in jar until ready to use. Remove onion after one day if dressing is not used up. Serve with green or fruit salads.

Yield: 2 cups

RED WINE YOGURT DRESSING

¼ cup red wine vinegar
¼ cup Dijon mustard
½ teaspoon salt

¾ cup olive oil
½ cup yogurt
2 teaspoons sugar

Mix vinegar, mustard and salt. Whisk in olive oil; add yogurt and sugar.

Yield: 1½ cups

1000 ISLAND DRESSING

3 hard-cooked eggs,
  chopped
¾ cup chili sauce
½ cup mayonnaise
1 tablespoon chopped
  parsley
1 cup sour cream

¼ cup chopped celery
1 (2-ounce) jar diced
  pimiento
1 tablespoon chopped
  yellow onion
  salt to taste

Mix all ingredients together and store in covered jar in the refrigerator. It will keep 2 to 3 weeks.

Yield: 3 cups

MUSTARD DRESSING

¼ cup mayonnaise
2 tablespoons red wine
  vinegar
1 tablespoon Dijon mustard
1 teaspoon salt

½ teaspoon sugar
1 cup olive oil
1 to 2 tablespoons fresh
  chopped parsley

Mix mayonnaise, vinegar, mustard, salt and sugar together. Gradually whisk in oil. Mix in parsley and refrigerate for several hours to blend flavors. Stir once again before serving.

Yield 1½ cups

POPPY SEED DRESSING

1 cup sugar
1 tablespoon dry mustard
1 teaspoon salt
¼ onion, finely grated

½ cup white vinegar
2 cups light olive oil
1½ tablespoons poppy seeds

Mix sugar, dry mustard, salt and onion very well. Add vinegar and mix well again. Slowly whisk in oil. Stir until dressing becomes thick and thoroughly mixed. Add poppy seeds. Serve on fruit salad or spinach greens.

Yield: 3 cups

SWEET AND SOUR DRESSING

⅓ cup sugar
1 teaspoon salt
1 teaspoon dry mustard

1 teaspoon onion juice (from finely minced onion)
⅓ cup cider vinegar
1 cup olive oil

Put all ingredients except oil in a blender. Add 1 tablespoon of oil and blend. Then gradually mix in rest of oil. Store at room temperature. This is best if used the day it is made. Refrigerate only if saving for another time; if so, it must be shaken well before using.

Yield: 1½ cups

UPSIDE DOWN DRESSING

½ teaspoon salt
2 cloves garlic, split
¼ cup fresh lemon juice
2 teaspoons Dijon mustard
¾ cup olive oil

¼ teaspoon pepper
2 uncooked eggs, parboiled for 10 full seconds
2 tablespoons drained and rinsed capers (optional)

Put salt in bottom of a large salad bowl. Rub the salt with the garlic to flavor it. Either mince the garlic and add to the dressing, or discard it as you prefer. Add the lemon juice, mustard, oil and pepper and blend thoroughly with a whisk. Add the eggs and whisk until the mixture looks creamy. Stir in the capers. Place salad ingredients in the bowl on top of the dressing. Do not toss. Cover with plastic wrap and refrigerate. Just before serving, toss salad until lettuce is well coated. Serve. This dressing may be made up to 8 hours ahead of serving.

Yield: ½ cup

SOUPS

The ruined entrance to
The Insurance Exchange on LaSalle Street.

SOUPS

STEWS

JALAPEÑO PUMPKIN SOUP

2 to 4 fresh jalapeño chilies,
   2½ to 3-inches long
2 tablespoons butter
1 small onion, chopped
½ teaspoon white pepper
½ teaspoon curry powder
1 large russet potato, peeled
   and cubed

2 medium carrots, peeled
   and cubed
¼ cup minced fresh parsley
4 cups chicken stock
1 (16-ounce) can pumpkin
⅓ cup good dry sherry

Stem, seed and mince chilies. Number of chilies used will determine piquancy of soup. Over medium heat, in a 4-quart saucepan, melt butter. Add onion and chilies, pepper and curry powder. Stir until onions are limp, about 5 minutes. Add potato, carrots, parsley and 2 cups of the stock. Bring to a boil; cover and reduce heat to simmer until the vegetables are very tender when pierced, about 20 minutes. Purée vegetable mixture in a blender until smooth. Return to pan. Stir in pumpkin, remaining stock and sherry. Stir over medium heat until hot. Serve immediately.

Yield: 4 to 6 servings

CREAM OF PEANUT SOUP

¼ cup butter
2 stalks celery, chopped
1 small onion, chopped
2 tablespoons all-purpose
   flour
2 cups chicken broth

1 cup milk
1 cup light cream
1 cup peanut butter
   salt, pepper and paprika
   to taste

In a 4-quart saucepan, brown celery and onions in butter. Add flour, chicken broth and milk; bring to a boil. Add cream and peanut butter and simmer for 5 minutes. Season to taste.

Yield: 6 to 8 cups

TOMATO, CUCUMBER AND AVOCADO SOUP

4 tablespoons butter
1 cup chopped onion
4 tablespoons all-purpose
   flour
4 cups peeled chopped
   tomatoes

4 cups peeled chopped
   cucumbers
4 cups chicken broth
   salt and pepper to taste
1 cup heavy cream
1 fresh ripe chopped
   avocado

Melt butter in a 4-quart saucepan or Dutch oven. Sauté onions until transparent. Add the flour and stir until thick. Add the tomatoes and using a wire whisk, combine them with the flour mixture. Add the cucumbers and whisk them in. Add chicken broth, salt and pepper. Combine well. Bring to a boil, reduce heat and simmer, uncovered, for 25 minutes. Pour a little soup at a time into a blender or food processor. Blend well and then strain. Chill soup. When ready to serve, add heavy cream and chopped avocado.

Yield: 8 to 10 servings

BLACK OLIVE SOUP

3 cups chicken stock
1 cup ripe black olives,
   pitted and sliced
1 tablespoon grated onion
1 clove garlic
2 eggs

1 cup half-and-half
1 teaspoon Worcestershire
   sauce
   salt to taste
   chopped parsley or basil
   to garnish

In a saucepan, simmer chicken stock with olives, onion and garlic for 10 to 15 minutes. Discard garlic. Beat together eggs and half-and-half. Slowly add a little of the stock to the egg mixture, stirring constantly. Add all the egg mixture to the stock, still stirring constantly. Heat until just before the boiling point but not at a boil. Season with Worcestershire sauce and salt. Serve hot or cold. Garnish with fresh herbs.

Yield: 4 to 6 servings

BROILED TOMATO SOUP

8	medium-sized fresh tomatoes or a (40-ounce) can Italian-style tomatoes, drained
½	cup butter
2	tablespoons olive oil
1	large onion, thinly sliced
½	teaspoon dried thyme
½	teaspoon dried basil
1	teaspoon fresh dill

3	tablespoons tomato paste
4	tablespoons all-purpose flour
3¾	cups chicken stock
	salt and pepper to taste
1	teaspoon sugar
1	cup whipping cream
½	cup grated Parmesan cheese

In a 4-quart saucepan, heat butter and olive oil; add the onion, thyme, basil and dill. Cook, stirring occasionally until onion is soft and golden. If using fresh tomatoes, peel and cut into small pieces. Add the tomatoes and tomato paste and stir to blend. Simmer, uncovered, for 10 minutes. In a small mixing bowl, blend flour and half of the chicken stock with a wire whisk. Add to the tomato and onion mixture. Add the remaining chicken stock and simmer, uncovered, for 30 minutes, stirring frequently down to the bottom of the pan to prevent scorching. Purée soup in a blender. Return to saucepan and add salt and pepper to taste. Reheat over low flame and add the sugar. Whip the cream and fold Parmesan cheese into it. Preheat broiler. Pour hot soup into individual oven-proof dishes or into a large ovenproof casserole dish. Float the whipped cream and Parmesan cheese mixture on top. Sprinkle with additional Parmesan cheese. Broil 6 inches from heat until golden brown, about 30 seconds to 1 minute. Watch closely so cream does not burn. Serve immediately.

Yield: 6 servings

BROCCOLI SOUP

1¾ pounds (8 cups) fresh broccoli	7 cups chicken stock salt and pepper to taste
2 Idaho potatoes	3 cups buttermilk
1½ tablespoons butter	½ teaspoon nutmeg
1 cup chopped onion	⅓ cup chopped fresh dill to garnish
½ teaspoon minced garlic	

Cut broccoli in small flowerets. Cut stems into ½-inch slices for a total of 8 cups of broccoli. Peel and cut potatoes into small chunks (approximately 2¾ cups). Heat butter in large saucepan; sauté chopped onion and garlic until onions are transparent; add chicken stock, salt and pepper and bring to a boil. Simmer, covered, 20 minutes or until potatoes are tender. Ladle mixture into a blender in small batches and purée. Return to pan or divide into several freezer containers for storage. When ready to use, reheat to simmer, then thin with buttermilk. Season with nutmeg. Garnish with fresh or dried dill. If freezing soup, do not add buttermilk until ready to use.

Yield: 8 to 12 servings

CURRIED SUMMER SQUASH SOUP

4 yellow squash	1 teaspoon cumin
2 tomatoes	1 tablespoon brown sugar salt and pepper to taste
½ onion	
3 cups chicken broth	½ cup rum
½ teaspoon curry	1 tablespoon butter
1 teaspoon nutmeg	

Chop squash, tomatoes and onion. Put vegetables in saucepan and add remaining ingredients. Bring all to a boil. Lower heat and simmer for 30 minutes. Transfer to a blender or food processor and purée. Chill if desired. Can be served either hot or cold.

Yield: 8 servings

CARROT SOUP

1 onion, chopped	2 potatoes, coarsely
3 small cloves garlic,	chopped
chopped	1 teaspoon salt
2 tablespoons butter	1 bay leaf
5 sprigs fresh thyme	white pepper to taste
or ½ teaspoon dried	¼ cup butter
4 cups chicken stock	fresh minced parsley to
6 carrots, coarsely chopped	garnish

In a large saucepan, sauté onion and garlic in 2 tablespoons butter until golden. Add thyme and sauté for a minute more. Add chicken stock, carrots, potatoes, salt, bay leaf and white pepper; simmer 30 minutes. Remove bay leaf and ladle into blender in small batches and purée. Return to pan and heat thoroughly. Swirl in ¼ cup butter. Garnish with minced parsley. For a low-fat variation, add 2 tablespoons tomato paste and 1 tablespoon white rice instead of potatoes. Use fresh cilantro to garnish.

Yield: 6 to 8 servings

CUCUMBER SOUP

2 large cucumbers	3 cups chicken broth
1 large Bermuda onion	salt and pepper to taste
2 tablespoons margarine	½ cup half-and-half
3 tablespoons all-purpose	fresh chive, dill or lemon
flour	slices to garnish

Slice and seed cucumbers. Peel and slice onion. In a large skillet, cook cucumbers and onion in margarine over moderate heat. Add flour and stir well. Add 2 cups chicken broth and cook for 15 minutes over moderate heat. Remove from heat; season to taste. Add remainder of chicken broth. Allow to cool, then put in a blender and purée. Pour contents through a strainer into a bowl. Stir in half-and-half and refrigerate until very cold. Serve in chilled bowls with fresh chive and/or dill sprinkled on top for garnish. Lemon slices are also a nice garnish.

Yield: 4 servings

SPINACH SOUP

3 cups chicken stock
1 cup warm water
1 cup chopped green onions
  including tops
1 potato, peeled and diced
2 (10-ounce) packages
  frozen chopped spinach
1 teaspoon sugar
½ teaspoon salt
1 teaspoon marjoram
¼ teaspoon fresh ground
  nutmeg
1½ tablespoons lemon juice
½ cup half-and-half or
  whipping cream
  croutons, sour cream or
  yogurt for garnish

In a large saucepan, combine stock, water, green onions and potato. Bring to a boil and simmer until potato is done, about 10 minutes. Stir in spinach, sugar, salt, marjoram, nutmeg and lemon juice. Bring to a simmer and cook until spinach is done, about 10 minutes; stir in cream. Transfer in small batches to blender and purée. Transfer to another saucepan and reheat to serving temperature. Garnish with croutons or a dollop of sour cream or plain yogurt. This recipe may either be prepared one day in advance of serving and refrigerated or frozen for up to 2 weeks. Also, Swiss chard may be substituted for either half or all of spinach.

Yield: 6 to 8 servings

SOUTHWESTERN CORN SOUP

2 (10-ounce) packages
   frozen corn, thawed
2 cups chicken stock
1 small onion, ¼-inch diced
1 medium carrot, ¼-inch
   diced
2 cloves garlic, chopped fine
1 teaspoon salt or to taste
1 teaspoon chili powder

½ teaspoon ground cumin
¼ teaspoon crushed red
   pepper
¼ teaspoon fresh ground
   black pepper
12 ounces milk
   fresh cilantro or ground
   coriander to garnish

Place thawed corn on a large cookie sheet and broil for about 5 minutes watching very closely and stirring occasionally to keep corn from sticking; cook until golden brown. While corn is roasting, combine chicken stock, onion, carrot, and garlic in a saucepan. Heat to boiling; reduce heat and simmer for 5 minutes. Add roasted corn, salt, chili powder, cumin, red pepper and black pepper. Cover and simmer 10 minutes. Place mixture in batches in blender and purée. Return to saucepan, add milk and heat to serving temperature. Garnish with fresh cilantro or ground coriander. This freezes well or can be made up to 1 day in advance of serving and refrigerated.

Yield: 4 to 6 servings

COLD SUMMER SOUP

1 bouquet garni (1 sprig each of parsley, marjoram and thyme, and 1 bay leaf tied in cheese cloth)
6 cups chicken stock
1 large shallot, diced
3 bunches green onions, chopped
¼ cup butter
4 (7-inch) sprigs mint

2 teaspoons chopped fresh tarragon
8 large fresh basil leaves
1½ teaspoons tarragon vinegar
2 (8-inch) cucumbers, coarsely chopped
1 medium tomato, seeded and chopped
½ pint whipping cream
salt and pepper to taste

In a large stock pan, place bouquet garni in chicken stock and boil gently for 20 minutes. In a large skillet, sauté shallot and green onions in butter about 5 minutes or until limp. Remove mint leaves from stems; discard stems. Chop mint leaves. Add tarragon, basil, vinegar, and cucumber, (reserving ¼ cup cucumber), and mint to shallot and green onion mixture. Sauté for about 5 minutes or until limp. Remove bouquet garni from stock. Add cucumber mixture to stock and allow to cool. Purée mixture in a blender or food processor a little at a time. Add chopped reserved cucumber, chopped tomato and cream. Chill well. Salt and pepper to taste.

Yield: 8 servings

LENTIL SOUP

½ pound bacon, chopped
½ pound sausage
2 cups chopped carrots
1 cup chopped onions
2 cups chopped celery
1 cup chopped leeks
2 cups dry lentils
2 tablespoons cider vinegar

6 cups chicken stock
6 cups beef stock
2 cloves garlic, minced
2 bay leaves
pepper to taste
½ teaspoon thyme
½ teaspoon marjoram

In a large pot, cook the bacon and sausage. Remove from the pot. In the same pot, cover and cook carrots, onions, celery and leeks for 5 minutes. Add lentils and vinegar. Cook for 8 minutes. Add chicken and beef stock, minced garlic, bay leaves, pepper, thyme and marjoram. Cook for 2 hours. Remove bay leaves and purée half of the volume. Return puréed mixture to pot; heat and serve.

Yield: 8 to 10 servings

WHITE GAZPACHO

1 cup salted sunflower seeds
2 cloves garlic, minced
¾ cup fresh bread crumbs, soaked in milk
½ cup olive oil
4 cups well-chilled chicken stock

3 tablespoons white wine vinegar
salt and white pepper to taste
garlic croutons
fresh chopped basil or sage to garnish

In a food processor or blender, grind sunflower seeds to a smooth paste. Add minced garlic. Drain bread crumbs and add to processor/blender contents. Blend until smooth. With processor/blender running, add olive oil, chicken stock and vinegar. Taste for seasoning; add salt and pepper to taste. Chill thoroughly. Serve with garlic croutons and fresh chopped herbs as garnish.

Yield: 4 servings

CHUNKY GAZPACHO

1 (46-ounce) can cocktail
  vegetable juice
1 chopped green pepper
3 fresh tomatoes, peeled
  and chopped
1 cucumber, peeled and
  chopped
1 small onion, chopped

2 teaspoons parsley
1 teaspoon chives
2 cloves garlic, pressed or
  ½ teaspoon garlic powder
2 tablespoons olive oil
  pepper and paprika to
  taste
10 dashes hot pepper sauce

Combine all ingredients. Refrigerate for several hours or over-night. Serve cold. If a smooth consistency is desired, run soup through blender or food processor to purée.

Yield: 8 servings

CHICKEN MINESTRONE

¼ cup vegetable oil
1 large onion, chopped
3 cloves garlic, chopped
2 celery stalks, diced
3 carrots, diced
2 zucchini, split and diced
2 large potatoes, diced
2 leeks, diced (optional)
4 ounces diced ham
2 quarts chicken stock
1 (12-ounce) can Italian
  tomatoes

1 tablespoon crushed dried
  basil
2 teaspoons salt
½ teaspoon pepper
1 cup cooked Great
  Northern beans
½ cup uncooked elbow
  macaroni or other small
  pasta
3 cups diced cooked
  chicken
  grated Parmesan cheese
  to garnish

Sauté onion and garlic in oil until golden and just beginning to brown. Add celery, carrots, zucchini, potatoes, leeks (if desired) and ham. Sauté for another 5 to 6 minutes. Add chicken stock, tomatoes, basil, salt and pepper; bring to a boil. Reduce heat and simmer for 2½ to 3 hours. Add beans, pasta and chicken. Simmer about 10 minutes or until pasta is tender. Salt and pepper to taste. Serve with grated Parmesan cheese and a nice loaf of crusty French bread.

Yield: 6 servings

MINNESOTA MINESTRONE

½ pound bacon, chopped
½ pound medium ham, diced
½ pound Italian sausage, sliced
6 cloves garlic, minced
1 large onion, chopped
6 quarts beef stock
1 (15-ounce) can red kidney beans, undrained
3 cups loosely shredded cabbage
1 cup medium-diced celery
1 leek, sliced
2 medium zucchini, sliced
2 cups Burgundy wine
1 teaspoon salt
½ teaspoon pepper
½ teaspoon allspice
1 (28-ounce) can Italian tomatoes, undrained
¼ cup fresh basil or 1 tablespoon dried
1 cup uncooked elbow macaroni

Lightly brown bacon, ham, sausage, garlic and onion in a Dutch oven or large skillet; drain. Heat stock in large soup kettle. Add bacon, ham, sausage, garlic and onion. Add beans, cabbage, celery, leek, zucchini, wine, salt, pepper and allspice. Simmer 45 minutes. Stir in tomatoes, basil and macaroni. Simmer about 15 minutes or until macaroni is tender. (May be frozen before adding macaroni).

Yield: 12 servings

TUSCAN BEAN SOUP

2 tablespoons olive oil
3 cloves garlic, minced
1 cup finely chopped green pepper
2 (13¾-ounce) cans chicken broth
1 cup canned crushed tomato
2 teaspoons crushed dried rosemary
2 (15½-ounce) cans Great Northern beans, drained and rinsed
½ cup chopped parsley pepper to taste

In a large pot, heat olive oil. Sauté garlic and green pepper in oil for 10 minutes or until soft. Add chicken broth, tomato and rosemary. Reduce heat and simmer for 20 minutes. Add beans and simmer for 10 minutes. Season with pepper and parsley.

Yield: 4 servings

ITALIAN SAUSAGE AND TORTELLINI SOUP

1 pound sweet Italian sausage	1 teaspoon oregano
1 cup (½-inch) sliced celery	1 teaspoon sugar
2 pounds (½-inch) sliced zucchini	½ teaspoon basil
1 cup chopped onion	2 cloves garlic, pressed
2 (28-ounce) cans crushed tomatoes	1½ cups red wine
1 teaspoon salt (optional)	1 cup water
1 teaspoon Italian seasoning	1 green pepper, diced
	1 (12-ounce) package frozen cheese tortellini
	small block Fontina cheese, grated

Remove casings from sausage. Brown in microwave or Dutch oven. Drain fat and crumble sausage. In stockpot, add celery to sausage and cook 10 minutes. Add zucchini, onion, crushed tomatoes, salt, Italian seasoning, oregano, sugar, basil, garlic, red wine and water; simmer for at least 20 minutes. Add green peppers and simmer for 10 minutes more. In a separate pan, cook tortellini according to package directions. Do not overcook as it will then lose shape in the soup. Add tortellini to soup. Add additional water or beef stock if necessary. Heat and serve. Sprinkle grated Fontina cheese on top. Mozzarella may be substituted if desired. If preparing soup ahead of time, do not add tortellini until just before reheating to serve.

Yield: 10 to 12 servings

ILLINOIS CHOWDER

3 tablespoons butter
2 medium onions, chopped
1 clove garlic, minced
3 cups chicken stock
2 cups whole milk
5 medium potatoes, peeled
  and diced
3 medium carrots, peeled
  and diced
5 cups fresh or frozen corn

⅓ cup fresh chopped basil or
  1 teaspoon dried
¾ teaspoon dry mustard
½ teaspoon fresh marjoram
  leaves
  salt and pepper to taste
1 cup whipping cream or
  half-and-half
3 to 4 chicken breasts,
  cooked, skinned and
  cubed

In a large heavy pot, over medium high heat, melt butter. Add onions and garlic. Sauté for 5 minutes or until onions are soft. Add stock, milk, potatoes, carrots, corn, basil, mustard and marjoram; salt and pepper to taste. Bring to a boil. Lower heat, cover, and simmer for about 20 minutes or until potatoes are tender. Using a slotted spoon, transfer 2 cups of vegetable mixture into a blender or food processor. Purée vegetables until smooth. Return to pot and stir to blend. Add cream or half-and-half to mixture in pot. Add cooked, cubed chicken. Bring soup to a boil over medium heat, stirring constantly. Lower heat and simmer for 5 to 8 minutes until flavors are well blended. Serve.

Yield: 8 servings

VEGETABLE CHOWDER

½ pound thinly sliced
zucchini
1 thinly sliced medium
onion
2 cups (32-ounce can)
tomatoes
1 pound can garbanzo
beans
4 tablespoons butter
2 cups white wine
2 teaspoons minced garlic
5 tablespoons finely
chopped parsley

1 teaspoon ground basil
1 bay leaf
¼ teaspoon ground sage
2 teaspoons salt
¼ teaspoon ground pepper
1 cup grated Monterey Jack
cheese
1 cup grated Romano
cheese
1 cup heavy cream
½ cup milk

Place all ingredients up to and including ground pepper in a large covered casserole dish. Bake in preheated 400° oven for 30 minutes. Stir. Continue baking another 30 minutes. Stir. Add cheeses, cream and milk. Reduce heat to 350° and continue baking, covered, for another 20 minutes.

Yield: 6 servings

QUICK FISH STOCK

4 green onions or 1 large
leek, thinly sliced
2 small onions, thinly sliced
3 cups bottled clam juice
2 cups water

¼ cup dry vermouth or dry
white wine
1 dried bay leaf
½ teaspoon thyme

Put all ingredients in a large non-aluminum saucepan. Bring to a boil and reduce. Heat and simmer, uncovered, for 30 minutes. Pour through a strainer into a non-metallic container. Can refrigerate for up to 3 days or freeze.

Yield: 5 cups

MUSSEL AND SAFFRON SOUP

4 tablespoons butter	1 clove garlic, finely minced
1 tablespoon salt	1 pound mussels
¾ teaspoon pepper	1½ pounds tomatoes, peeled,
1 bay leaf	seeded, juiced and
¼ teaspoon thyme	roughly chopped
1 large (approximately	2¼ cups fish stock
½ pound) onion, finely	½ cup heavy cream
minced	½ teaspoon saffron
½ leek (white part only),	salt and freshly ground
finely minced	pepper to taste
1 large carrot, finely	
minced	

In a heavy 4-quart saucepan, melt the butter over low heat. When completely melted, add salt, pepper, bay leaf, thyme, onion, leek, carrot and garlic. Continue cooking, covered, over low heat for 20 minutes, or until the vegetables reduce nearly to a purée. Be careful not to scorch the vegetables. While the vegetables are cooking, scrub the mussels clean, pulling off their beards. In a large stock pot, bring ½-inch of water to a boil. Drop in the mussels, cover, and steam them over high heat until they open, about 3 minutes. Drain the mussels and rinse them under cold running water. Discard any mussels that have not opened. Remove the mussels from their shells, pulling off any beards you may have missed the first time. In a small bowl, place the cooked mussels in just enough water to cover. Cover the bowl and refrigerate until you are ready to use them. After the vegetables have stewed, add tomatoes and cook, uncovered, over moderate heat for another 20 minutes, or until the tomatoes have reduced nearly to a purée. Add the fish stock. Bring the mixture to a boil and simmer for another 10 minutes. Remove the bay leaf. Add the cream, saffron, drained reserved mussels and more salt and pepper if necessary. Simmer the soup for 5 minutes, or until hot. This soup ages nicely and tastes even better when made the day before it is served. The consistency is never smooth, as the vegetables are not puréed into the body of the soup. Serve in hot soup bowls or soup plates and grind fresh pepper onto the center of each serving.

Yield: 4 to 6 servings

CINCINNATI CHILI

4 cups water
2 (8-ounce) cans tomato sauce
2 cups chopped onion
2 tablespoons chili powder
2 tablespoons vinegar
2 teaspoons Worcestershire sauce
2 teaspoons ground cinnamon
1 teaspoon salt
1 teaspoon cumin
½ teaspoon allspice
¼ teaspoon ground cloves
¼ teaspoon garlic powder
½ ounce unsweetened chocolate
1 bay leaf
1 dried red chili pepper
2 pounds lean ground beef
1 pound spaghetti, cooked
chopped onion (optional)
shredded cheese (optional)
kidney beans (optional)

In 4-quart Dutch oven, combine all ingredients except ground beef. Bring to boiling. Crumble meat and add slowly to liquid; return to boiling. Reduce heat and simmer 2 to 3 hours, uncovered, until thickened as desired. Remove bay leaf and chili pepper. Serve over spaghetti. Top with chopped onion, shredded cheese and/or kidney beans.

Yield: 8 to 10 servings

WHITE BEAN CHILI

1 pound dried Great Northern white beans	¼ teaspoon ground cloves
2 pounds ground turkey	¼ teaspoon cayenne pepper
1 tablespoon olive oil	6 cups chicken stock or canned broth
2 medium onions, chopped	3 cups grated Monterey Jack cheese
4 cloves garlic, minced	
2 (4-ounce) cans chopped mild green chilies	salt and pepper to taste
2 teaspoons ground cumin	sour cream to garnish
1½ teaspoons dried oregano, crumbled	salsa to garnish
	chopped fresh cilantro to garnish

Rinse beans and sort out any bad ones. Place beans in large heavy pot. Add enough cold water to cover by at least 3-inches and soak overnight. Cook turkey in a large heavy saucepan until cooked through; set aside. Drain beans. Heat oil in same pot used for beans over medium high heat. Add onions and sauté until translucent, about 10 minutes. Stir in garlic, then chilies, cumin, oregano, ground cloves, and cayenne pepper; sauté for 2 minutes. Add beans and stock and bring to boil. Reduce heat and simmer until beans are very tender, stirring occasionally, for about 2 hours. Add turkey and 1 cup grated cheese and stir until cheese melts. Season to taste with salt and pepper. Ladle chili into bowls. Serve with remaining cheese, sour cream, salsa and cilantro.

Yield: 8 servings

BLACK BEAN CHILI

1 tablespoon cumin seed	4 cloves garlic, minced
1 tablespoon dried oregano	4 tomatoes, peeled, seeded and chopped
2 teaspoons sweet paprika	
½ teaspoon cayenne pepper	2 cups dried black beans, rinsed and cleaned
1 (4-ounce) can hot green chilies, diced	1 bay leaf
3 tablespoons corn oil	3 cups water
1 chopped onion	¼ cup chopped fresh coriander leaves
1½ teaspoons salt	
3 tablespoons chili powder	8 slices Muenster cheese
1 green bell pepper, chopped	1 cup sour cream to garnish

In a small dry skillet, toast the cumin seed, oregano, paprika and cayenne pepper over moderately high heat, stirring for 2 minutes or until the paprika turns several shades darker. Transfer to a bowl and add the green chilies. In a Dutch oven, heat the corn oil, and sauté the onion for 5 minutes. Add ½ teaspoon salt, green chili mixture, chili powder, bell pepper, garlic and tomatoes. Simmer the mixture for 15 minutes. Add black beans, bay leaf and water. Cook partially covered, over low heat for 2 to 2½ hours or until the beans are tender. Add more water if necessary while beans are cooking. Stir in the coriander and the remaining teaspoon salt. Place 1 slice of the Muenster cheese in each of 8 bowls. Ladle the chili over the cheese and garnish with some of the sour cream.

Yield: 8 servings

TEXAS CHILI

2 pounds beef brisket
1 large onion
1 green pepper
2 jalapeño peppers with
   seeds
1 clove garlic
2 tablespoons chili powder
1 tablespoon paprika
½ teaspoon oregano
½ teaspoon ground cumin
½ teaspoon crushed red
   pepper
   dash hot pepper sauce
   pinch of sugar
1 (32-ounce) can tomatoes
1 (8-ounce) can tomato
   sauce
½ cup beef broth
½ cup flat beer

In tightly covered Dutch oven, cook meat for 2 hours at 350°. Remove all fat from meat and drippings. (Chill overnight and fat will be easy to remove from gravy.) Chop onion, green pepper, jalapeños and garlic. Sauté. Stir in chili powder, paprika, oregano, cumin, red pepper, hot pepper sauce and a pinch of sugar. Add the tomatoes and juice, tomato sauce, broth, beer and meat. Cover and simmer for 1 hour. Uncover and cook for 2 more hours, stirring frequently. Refrigerate overnight or up to 2 days. Reheat and serve.

Yield: 6 to 8 servings

BEEF STEW

1½ to 2 pounds cubed beef;
    chuck or round
3 to 4 carrots, peeled and
   chopped
3 to 4 medium potatoes,
   peeled and diced
1 cup chopped celery
1 large onion, quartered
2 cups canned tomatoes
1 cup tomato sauce
1 clove garlic, peeled
3 tablespoons minute
   tapioca
1 tablespoon brown sugar
½ cup red wine
   salt and pepper to taste
1 (6.5-ounce) can water
   chestnuts, drained

Combine all ingredients, except water chestnuts, in a covered casserole dish. Bake at 250° for 5 hours. Add water chestnuts during last 15 minutes of baking.

Yield: 4 to 6 servings

LAMB AND ARTICHOKE STEW

4 tablespoons butter
2 pounds boneless lamb, cubed
3 medium yellow onions
2 cloves garlic, crushed
1 cup chopped parsley
  salt and pepper to taste

1 (6-ounce) can tomato paste
1 cup dry white wine
2 (14-ounce) cans artichoke hearts, drained
½ teaspoon dried dill
3 tablespoons lemon juice

Melt butter in skillet. Add the lamb and sauté until lightly browned. Remove the meat from the skillet. Peel and chop the onions. Sauté onion, garlic and parsley in same skillet with remaining butter. Place meat, onions, garlic and parsley in large kettle. Add tomato paste, white wine and salt and pepper to taste. Simmer, covered, for about 1½ hours or until lamb is tender. Add the artichoke hearts, dill and lemon juice. Simmer, covered, again until all is tender, about 1½ hours more. Serve over rice. This stew freezes well.

Yield: 4 servings

BALLYMALOE IRISH STEW

4 tablespoons butter
3 pounds shoulder lamb chops
4 quartered carrots
8 to 10 tiny onions

2½ cups beef broth
6 small potatoes, peeled
1 tablespoon fresh parsley
1 tablespoon fresh chives
  salt and pepper to taste

Heat 3 tablespoons butter in large pot. When butter has melted, brown the chops; set aside. When all are browned, return them to the pot. Add carrots, onions and beef broth. Put potatoes on top. Cover stew and simmer about 2 hours. With a slotted spoon, transfer meat and vegetables to bowls. Skim the fat. Swirl in remaining butter and herbs and ladle sauce over the meat and vegetables.

Yield: 6 servings

DESSERTS

The Chicago Water Tower survived the fire.

DESSERTS

KAHLUA WHITE RUSSIAN CAKE

Cake:

3 tablespoons Kahlua	½ cup butter
2 tablespoons vodka	2 tablespoons shortening
½ cup (3-ounces) white chocolate	1¼ cups sugar
	3 eggs
2 cups sifted cake flour	¾ cup buttermilk
¾ teaspoon baking soda	⅓ cup apricot jam
¼ teaspoon baking powder	

Frosting:

2 cups heavy cream	⅓ cup Kahlua
⅓ cup sifted powdered sugar	2 teaspoons vodka

To make the cake, grease well and flour lightly two 9-inch cake pans. Combine Kahlua, vodka and chocolate in medium saucepan and put on low heat until chocolate melts, stirring to blend. Cool slightly. Re-sift cake flour, baking soda and baking powder into medium bowl and set aside. In large mixing bowl, cream together butter, sugar and shortening until light and fluffy. Beat in eggs 1 at a time. Blend in Kahlua-chocolate mixture. Then blend in flour mixture alternately with buttermilk. Divide batter between two pans and bake at 350° for 25 to 30 minutes or until toothpick inserted in center comes out clean. Cool in pans 10 minutes, then turn out onto wire racks until completely cool. Spread bottom surface of one cake layer with half the jam and ¼ cup frosting. Spread bottom surface of second layer with remaining jam. Place on top of first layer. Swirl remaining frosting on top and sides. Refrigerate. Remove 30 minutes before serving.

To make frosting, beat heavy cream and sugar with an electric mixer until thickened. Gradually beat in Kahlua and vodka and continue beating until stiff.

Yield: 10 servings

CHOCOLATE RASPBERRY PASTRY CAKE

Pastry Cake:

1 cup (6-ounces) semi-
   sweet chocolate chips
½ cup sugar
½ cup water
¼ teaspoon cinnamon
2 teaspoons vanilla extract

1 package (9 or 10-ounce)
   pie crust mix or
   homemade pie crust
2 cups whipping cream
2 cups fresh raspberries

Raspberry Sauce:

1 pint fresh raspberries
½ cup superfine instant
   dissolving sugar

1 to 2 tablespoons fresh
   lemon juice

To make cake, in a small saucepan melt chocolate chips, sugar, water and cinnamon over low heat, stirring frequently until chips are melted and mixture is smooth. Remove from heat. Add vanilla and cool to room temperature. Blend ¾ cup chocolate sauce into pie crust mix. Divide crust mixture into 4 parts. Press or spread each part over the bottom of an inverted 8-inch round cake pan to within ¼ inch of the edge. Bake all 4 pastry shells in a 425° oven for 8 to 10 minutes, or until pastry is firm. Remove from the oven. If necessary, trim edges with a sharp knife. Cool pastry layers. Run the tip of a knife under the edges of layers to loosen them from the pans. Lift layers very carefully since they are fragile. Whip the cream until it begins to hold soft peaks. Fold in the remaining chocolate sauce. Spread between torte layers and over the top. Chill at least 8 hours. Before serving, cover entire top of cake with raspberries. Ladle a pool of raspberry sauce on individual plates. Place a slice of cake on top of sauce.

To make the sauce, wash berries well and puree in blender. Add sugar to taste. Blend until dissolved. Add lemon juice and blend until all sugar granules are dissolved. Put through a sieve to strain out seeds.

Yield: 9 to 12 servings

CHOCOLATE POUND CAKE

2 sticks margarine	½ teaspoon baking powder
4 tablespoons shortening	½ teaspoon salt
3 cups sugar	¾ cup cocoa
5 eggs	1 cup milk
3 cups sifted all-purpose flour	1 teaspoon vanilla extract

Beat margarine, shortening and sugar until light and fluffy. Beat in eggs, one at a time. Sift together flour, baking powder, salt and cocoa. Add vanilla to milk. Alternating between the flour mixture and milk, add to the shortening mixture. Pour into a greased tube pan. Bake at 325° for 1 hour and 20 minutes.

Yield: 8 to 10 servings

GERMAN PEACH CAKE

⅓ cup butter or margarine	1 tablespoon cornstarch
2 tablespoons sugar	⅛ teaspoon salt
1 cup all-purpose flour	⅛ teaspoon nutmeg
1 egg, slightly beaten	8 large peaches, peeled, pitted and sliced
½ teaspoon baking powder	
1 cup sugar	1 cup sour cream
¼ teaspoon cinnamon	¼ cup sugar

Mix together butter, sugar, flour, egg and baking powder as if for a pie crust and pat with hands into a 9-inch square pan. In a large bowl, combine sugar, cinnamon, cornstarch, salt and nutmeg. Add peach slices and toss. Arrange peach slices in rows on dough. Sprinkle any remaining sugar mixture in bowl on top of peaches. In a medium bowl, mix together the sour cream and remaining ¼ cup sugar. Pour over peaches. Bake in a 350° oven for 35 minutes. Serve warm or cold.

Yield: 6 servings

BLUEBERRY CAKE

Cake:

6	tablespoons (¾ stick) unsalted butter, softened	½	cup milk
¾	cup sugar	2	cups flour
1	large egg	2	teaspoons baking powder
1	teaspoon vanilla extract	½	teaspoon salt
		2	cups blueberries

Topping:

½	cup sugar	¼	cup (½ stick) unsalted butter
⅓	cup all-purpose flour		
¾	teaspoon cinnamon		

To make the cake, preheat oven to 375°. In a large bowl, cream together butter and sugar. Add egg and vanilla and beat until the mixture is well combined. Stir in milk. In a separate bowl, sift together flour, baking powder and salt. Stir into the creamed mixture and fold in blueberries. Spoon into a well-buttered 9-inch square baking pan and smooth the top.

To make the topping, blend sugar, flour and cinnamon in a bowl. Cut in the butter with a pastry blender or fork until the mixture is crumbly. Sprinkle evenly over the batter and bake at 375° for 45 minutes or until toothpick inserted in center comes out clean. Cool, cut into squares and serve warm.

Yield: 6 servings

BLUEBERRY PEACH CAKE

2 tablespoons cinnamon
7 tablespoons sugar
3 teaspoons baking powder
3 cups all-purpose flour
2 cups sugar
⅔ cup vegetable oil
4 eggs

2½ teaspoons vanilla extract
⅓ cup orange juice
1 pint blueberries, washed and drained
2 (16-ounce) cans sliced peaches, drained

Mix together cinnamon and sugar and set aside. Place baking powder, flour, sugar, oil, eggs, vanilla and orange juice in mixing bowl. Beat at low speed for 5 minutes. Batter will be very thick. Grease and flour tube pan. Layer batter, then fruit, then cinnamon-sugar combination into pan. This makes 3 layers. Bake for 1½ hours at 350°. Remove from oven and cool in pan on rack for 1 hour. Remove cake from the pan but do not cut the cake for 5 to 8 hours.

Yield: 8 to 10 servings

RHUBARB CAKE

½ cup butter
1½ cups sugar
1 egg
2½ cups all-purpose flour
1 teaspoon baking soda
½ teaspoon salt

1 cup milk
1 teaspoon vanilla extract
2 cups chopped rhubarb
½ cup sugar
1 teaspoon cinnamon

Cream together butter and sugar; add egg. In a separate bowl, combine flour, soda and salt, set aside. In another bowl, combine milk and vanilla. Add dry ingredients to creamed mixture alternately with milk mixture, blending well. Fold in chopped rhubarb. Pour in a 13 x 9 x 2-inch pan. Mix together sugar and cinnamon; sprinkle on top. Bake at 350° for 35 to 45 minutes. Serve warm or cool.

Yield: 10 to 12 servings

ORANGE CAKE

Cake:

8 eggs, separated	¼ cup orange juice
¼ teaspoon salt	1 cup plus 2 level
1 teaspoon cream of tartar	tablespoons cake flour,
1⅓ cups sugar	sifted
1 grated orange rind	

Filling:

¾ cup sugar	1 egg
juice and rind of 1 orange	½ pint heavy cream,
3 tablespoons all-purpose flour	whipped

Icing:

1 egg yolk	1 tablespoon cream
2 cups powdered sugar	2 tablespoons orange juice
4 tablespoons butter	

To make the cake, beat egg whites with salt until foamy. Add cream of tartar and beat until stiff. Gradually add ⅔ cup of sugar. In a separate bowl, beat egg yolks until thick. Add remaining sugar to egg yolks and beat again. Add orange juice and rind to yolk mixture. Slowly fold into egg whites. Sift flour over the mixture and fold in carefully. Pour into angel food pan and bake 1 hour at 325°. Invert pan and let cool 24 hours. Cut cake into three layers.

To prepare the filling, cook sugar, juice and rind of 1 orange, flour and egg in a double boiler, stirring constantly until thick; cool. Fold into 1 pint of whipped cream. Spread on inside layers of cake.

To make the icing, mix all ingredients well. Frost top and sides of the cake.

Yield: 8 to 10 servings

DATE ORANGE CAKE

Cake:

2⅓ cups sifted all-purpose
flour
½ teaspoon salt
1 teaspoon baking soda
1 teaspoon baking powder
1 cup butter, softened
2 cups sugar

2 eggs
1 cup chopped nuts
1 cup cut-up dates
grated rinds of 2 oranges
1 cup buttermilk
1 teaspoon vinegar
juice of 2 oranges

Icing:

1 cup butter
juice of 2 oranges

grated rind of 1 orange
4 cups powdered sugar

To make the cake, in a large bowl sift together flour, salt, baking soda and baking powder; set aside. In a separate bowl, cream together butter and 1 cup of sugar; add eggs and beat well, set aside. In another bowl, sprinkle a little flour over nuts and dates, reserve. Add rind to creamed mixture. Into creamed butter mixture, alternately stir in dry ingredients, buttermilk and vinegar. Mix well. Add nuts and dates. Turn into greased tube pan and bake at 350° for 25 minutes or until done. When done, remove cake from oven but leave in pan. Combine orange juice and 1 cup sugar and pour over cake. Leave in pan until cool.

To prepare the icing, beat butter until fluffy. Gradually add orange juice, orange rind and sugar. Thin with enough orange juice until consistency is correct. Remove cake from pan when cool and ice the cake.

Yield: 8 to 10 servings

ORANGE GINGERBREAD

½ cup butter or margarine
½ cup light brown sugar
½ cup light molasses
1 egg, beaten
1 orange, juice and rind

½ cup strong cold tea
1¾ cups all-purpose flour
¾ teaspoon baking soda
1 teaspoon ginger

Cream together butter and sugar. Add molasses, beaten egg, juice and grated rind of orange. Beat well. Add tea and flour sifted with soda and ginger. Bake in greased and floured 8 x 8-inch pan for 30 minutes at 350°.

Yield: 6 to 8 servings

APPLE CHEESECAKE

½ cup butter
⅔ cup sugar plus ¼ cup sugar
1 cup all-purpose flour
1 (8-ounce) package cream cheese, softened
1 egg

½ teaspoon vanilla extract
½ teaspoon cinnamon
4 cups sliced peeled apples
1 (8-ounce) jar apricot jam
¼ cup water
¾ cup sliced almonds, toasted in butter

Cream together butter with ⅓ cup sugar. Gradually add in flour, stirring as you add. Spread and pat onto bottom of 9-inch springform pan. Pat dough about 1½ inches up sides of spring-form pan. Combine softened cream cheese with ¼ cup sugar beating well on low speed. Add egg and vanilla. Beat until smooth. Pour into pastry-lined pan. In a separate bowl, combine ⅓ cup sugar with ½ teaspoon cinnamon and toss apples in sugar-cinnamon mixture. Arrange slices over cream cheese. Bake at 350° for 30 to 35 minutes. While cake is baking, prepare apricot glaze by mixing jam with ¼ cup water. Simmer for 5 minutes and press through a strainer. Cool until thick enough to glaze cake. When cake and glaze have cooled fully, spread cake with apricot glaze and sprinkle with toasted slivered almonds.

Yield: 6 to 8 servings

PINEAPPLE CHEESECAKE

12 Zwieback crackers	1 cup sugar
2 tablespoons butter, melted	3 eggs
2 tablespoons sugar	1½ teaspoons vanilla extract
1 (20-ounce) can crushed pineapple	1 pint sour cream
3 (8-ounce) packages cream cheese	3 tablespoons sugar
	1 teaspoon vanilla extract

Crush Zwieback crackers and add 2 tablespoons sugar and butter. Mix thoroughly and spread and pat down all but 2 tablespoons in bottom of 8-inch springform pan. Drain pineapple; set aside. In a separate bowl, beat cream cheese, eggs, sugar and vanilla. Fold in pineapple. Pour into crust. Bake for 20 minutes at 375°. Remove from oven and turn temperature up to 500°. Whip together sour cream, sugar and vanilla. Pour on top of cake; sprinkle reserved Zwieback crumbs on top and return to oven and bake for 5 minutes. Cool cake and then refrigerate for at least 5 hours or longer. It is best to prepare cake the day before it is to be served. To serve with a raspberry sauce, purée a box of thawed frozen raspberries with sugar.

Yield: 8 servings

PINEAPPLE NUT CAKE

Cake:

2 cups all-purpose flour	2 teaspoons baking soda
2 cups crushed drained pineapple	2 eggs
2 cups sugar	1 cup walnuts

Frosting:

1 (8-ounce) package cream cheese	1 tablespoon vanilla extract
½ cup butter, softened	1½ to 2 cups powdered sugar

To make the cake, grease and flour a 13 x 9 x 2-inch pan. Stir all ingredients together and pour into pan. Bake about 40 minutes at 350°.

To make the frosting, cream butter and cream cheese until light. Add vanilla and sugar to make a spreadable icing. Frost the cake.

Yield: 10 to 12 servings

POTATO CAKE

2 cups sugar	2 teaspoons baking powder
⅔ cup butter	4 eggs
1 cup hot mashed potatoes	1 teaspoon cinnamon
2 squares bitter chocolate, melted	1 teaspoon ground cloves
½ cup milk	½ teaspoon grated nutmeg
2 cups all-purpose flour	1 cup chopped walnuts or pecans

Preheat oven to 325°. In a large mixing bowl, cream together sugar and butter until light. Add potatoes, chocolate, milk. Into this sift together flour and baking powder. Add eggs one at a time, beating well after each addition. Thoroughly stir in cinnamon, cloves and nutmeg. Fold in nuts. Pour into a well-greased 9-inch springform pan. Bake about 35 minutes or until cake springs back when touched. Remove from pan when cool. Spread with icing of choice.

Yield: 6 to 8 servings

PRUNE CAKE

Cake:

2 cups all-purpose flour	1 cup vegetable oil
½ teaspoon salt	1 teaspoon vanilla extract
1 teaspoon baking soda	1 cup buttermilk
1 teaspoon cinnamon	1 cup cooked chopped
1½ cups sugar	prunes
¼ teaspoon baking soda	1 cup chopped walnuts
3 eggs	

Sauce:

1 stick of butter	½ cup buttermilk
1 cup sugar	¼ teaspoon vanilla extract
¼ teaspoon baking soda	

To make the cake, into a medium mixing bowl, sift together flour, salt, baking soda and cinnamon; set aside. In a separate bowl, mix together eggs, oil, vanilla and buttermilk; combine with the flour mixture and mix well. Fold in prunes and nuts. Bake in a greased and floured 13 x 9 x 2-inch pan at 350° for 45 minutes.

To make the sauce, while cake is baking, in a 2-quart saucepan, melt butter together with sugar, baking soda, buttermilk and vanilla over low heat until sugar is dissolved. Pour over cake when it is removed from the oven.

Yield: 8 to 10 servings

OLD-FASHIONED FRUIT CAKE

4	ounces candied fruit peels	
4	ounces mixed red and green candied cherries	
4	ounces candied pineapple	
16	ounces dates	
¼	cup all-purpose flour	
1	cup butter or margarine	
½	cup sugar	
½	cup honey	
5	eggs, well beaten	

1½	cups all-purpose flour
1	teaspoon baking powder
½	teaspoon ground cloves
1	teaspoon salt
1	teaspoon ground allspice
½	teaspoon nutmeg
¼	cup orange juice
	brandy or rum (optional)
	chopped nuts (optional)

Shred fruit peels and halve cherries. Cut up pineapple and dates into almond size pieces. In a separate bowl, dredge fruit in ¼ cup flour; set aside. Cream together butter and sugar. Add honey, then eggs and beat well. Into creamed mixture, sift together remaining flour with baking powder, ground cloves, salt, ground allspice and nutmeg alternately adding orange juice in small amounts and mixing thoroughly each time. Pour the batter over the floured fruit and mix well. Line greased loaf pans with wax paper or brown paper; grease paper also. Allow ½-inch of paper to extend above sides of the pans. Pour the batter into pans. Do not flatten. Bake in slow oven (250°) for 3 to 4 hours. While baking, place pan containing 2 cups of water on bottom shelf of oven. This gives greater volume, a moister texture and a smooth shiny glaze. If decoration of nuts and fruit is desired, place on cakes after 2 hours in oven. After cakes are baked and cooled, if desired, pour a small amount of brandy and/or rum over cakes and wrap cakes in cotton cloth soaked in same. Wrap each cake in heavy aluminum foil. Store in refrigerator while cakes imbibe. Soak cloth each day for several days to give cakes a wonderful flavor. Don't add too much liquid at a time or cakes will become crumbly.

Yield: 2 loaves

MINIATURE EGGNOG CUPCAKES

Cupcakes:

½ cup butter or margarine
1½ cups sugar
2 eggs
3 cups all-purpose flour
3 teaspoons baking powder

½ teaspoon salt
2 cups eggnog
1 cup finely chopped candied fruit (cherries, etc.)

Frosting:

1½ cups powdered sugar
¼ teaspoon nutmeg
¼ teaspoon cinnamon

3 tablespoons eggnog candied red and green cherries

To make cupcakes, cream together butter and sugar. Add eggs, one at a time, beating well. Add flour sifted together with baking powder and salt alternately with eggnog. Fold in candied fruits. Spoon into paper-lined miniature muffin pans, 1¾-inch in diameter, about ¾ full. Bake at 350° about 25 minutes until very lightly browned.

To make frosting, blend all ingredients together until smooth. Spread a small amount on each cupcake and top with slivers of red and green cherries.

Yield: 12 large or 24 small cupcakes

CREAM CHEESE ICING

1   (8-ounce) package cream
    cheese
2½ cups powdered sugar

1   stick butter
2   teaspoons vanilla extract

Beat all ingredients together and spread on cake when cool.

Yield: Enough for one sheet cake

FUDGE ICING

3   cups sugar
1   cup milk
3   tablespoons corn syrup
2   squares chocolate

¼   teaspoon salt
¼   cup butter
1   teaspoon vanilla extract

Butter sides of a 3-quart saucepan. Combine sugar, milk, syrup, chocolate and salt. Cook and stir until chocolate and sugar are melted. Cook to soft ball stage (234°) without stirring. Remove from heat and add butter. Cool to 110°. Add vanilla. Beat until spreading consistency.

Yield: Enough for one sheet cake

SEVEN MINUTE ICING

2   egg whites, unbeaten
¾   cup sugar
2   tablespoons water
⅓   cup corn syrup

¼   teaspoon cream of tartar
¼   teaspoon salt
1   teaspoon vanilla extract

Combine all ingredients. Mix thoroughly. Place in top of double boiler over rapidly boiling water, beating constantly while cooking. Cook until frosting stands in peaks, about 7 minutes. Remove from water. Add vanilla and spread on cake.

Yield: Enough for one sheet cake

BUTTERSCOTCH BANANA PIE

Filling:

1 9-inch baked pie crust
3 tablespoons all-purpose flour
3 tablespoons cornstarch
2 tablespoons sugar
2 egg yolks

1½ cups firmly packed light brown sugar
1½ cups cold water
3 tablespoons butter
⅛ teaspoon salt
1 teaspoon pure vanilla extract

Topping:

3 large bananas, peeled and sliced in rounds
½ pint whipping cream

2 tablespoons sugar
¼ teaspoon pure vanilla extract

To make the filling, sift together flour, cornstarch and sugar into a medium-sized mixing bowl; set aside. In small mixing bowl, beat egg yolks lightly with a fork; set aside. In heavy 2-quart saucepan heat brown sugar and water over moderate heat, stirring occasionally until boiling. When at the boiling point, pour over flour mixture and blend with a spoon. Put entire mixture back into pan over moderate heat and continue to cook, stirring constantly until thick. Remove from heat. Add a small portion of hot mixture from pan to egg yolks. Blend and return contents of entire bowl to pan. Cook filling over moderate heat for 1 more minute. Remove from heat and add butter, salt and vanilla. Cool. When cold, pour butterscotch filling into cooled baked pie crust; chill.

For the topping, just before serving, peel and slice the bananas in rounds and place on top of the butterscotch. Whip cream until stiff. Add 2 tablespoons sugar and ¼ teaspoon vanilla extract. Cover entire pie with sweetened whipped cream.

Yield: 6 servings

SOUR CREAM APPLE PIE

Pie and Crust:

3 tablespoons melted butter	¾ cup sugar
1½ cups graham cracker crumbs	1 egg
¼ teaspoon ground cinnamon	1 cup sour cream
2 tablespoons all-purpose flour	½ teaspoon vanilla extract
⅛ teaspoon salt	2 cups sliced Granny Smith apples
	½ cup raisins

Topping:

⅓ cup sugar	⅓ cup all-purpose flour
¾ teaspoon ground nutmeg	¼ cup butter

To make the pie and crust, preheat oven to 350°. Melt butter. Pour graham cracker crumbs into a bowl and add melted butter and cinnamon. Mix well and pour into pie pan. Shape crust in pie pan until firm; place in refrigerator. Sift together flour, salt and sugar into a large mixing bowl. Add egg to sifted ingredients; mix together. Add sour cream and vanilla extract; mix well. Add apples and raisins. Pour into unbaked graham cracker crust. Bake for 30 minutes in a 350° oven. Remove pie and increase oven temperature to 400°.

For the topping, mix together sugar, nutmeg, flour and butter until crumbly. Sprinkle topping over apples. Return to oven and bake for another 10 minutes.

Yield: 6 to 8 servings

BLUEBERRY PEACH PIE

Crust:

2 cups all-purpose flour
1 teaspoon salt

⅔ cup plus 2 tablespoons shortening
3 to 5 tablespoons ice water

Filling:

¾ cup sugar
⅓ cup flour
1½ teaspoons ground cinnamon
2½ to 3 cups fresh blueberries

2 cups fresh peeled and sliced peaches
ice cream or whipped cream to garnish

To make the crust, mix together flour and salt. Cut in ½ of the shortening with a pastry blender or 2 knives until mixture resembles coarse crumbs. Cut in remaining shortening. Sprinkle with ice water and mix lightly with a fork until a ball forms. Roll out ⅔'s of the dough on a floured surface in a circle to fit a 9-inch pie pan. Ease dough into the pan leaving overhang untrimmed.

Preheat oven to 425°. Mix sugar, flour and cinnamon in a large bowl. Add fruit and mix well. Pour into pie shell. Roll out remaining dough and cover pie. Pinch edges tightly to seal and flute edges. Cut vents in top for steam to escape. Bake until crust is lightly browned, 40 to 50 minutes. Cool on wire rack at least 10 minutes before serving. Delicious with ice cream or whipped cream.

Yield: 6 to 8 servings

UPSIDE DOWN APPLE TART

½ cup butter, softened	vanilla ice cream
½ to 1 cup sugar	(optional)
4 pounds tart cooking	sweetened whipped
apples or fresh peaches	cream or crème fraîche
1 10-inch pie crust	(optional)

Coat the inside of a 10-inch ovenproof deep dish pie plate with a thick layer of softened butter. Cover the butter with a ¼-inch layer of sugar. Peel, core and thinly slice 4 pounds tart cooking apples; fill the pie pan with apples. Sprinkle with a little more sugar and dot with butter. Cover the whole dish with a single pie crust, crimping the edges to the plate. Bake in a 375° oven for about 30 minutes. Test to see if the apples are golden and the sugar is beginning to caramelize by carefully lifting the crust and peeking under it. When sugar caramelizes, loosen the crust from around the edges and cover the dish with a large serving platter. Turn the pie over onto the platter in one swift motion, as in unmolding a gelatin mold. Serve warm with ice cream, whipped cream or crème fraîche.

Yield: 8 servings

RUM AND PEACH PIE

3½ cups peeled and sliced	½ teaspoon ground
fresh peaches	cinnamon
¾ cup sugar	butter or margarine
2 tablespoons all-purpose	pastry dough for pie crust
flour	and top
3 tablespoons rum	

In a large mixing bowl, mix together peaches, sugar, flour, rum and cinnamon; place in an unbaked pie shell. Dot with butter. Make a lattice top out of pie pastry and crimp edges of top and crust together. Sprinkle top with extra sugar and cinnamon. Bake in a 375° oven for 40 to 50 minutes until golden brown and bubbly.

Yield: 6 to 8 servings

FAUX KEY LIME PIE

12 graham crackers
4 tablespoons sugar
7 tablespoons butter, chilled and thinly sliced
5 large egg yolks
1 (14-ounce) can sweetened condensed milk
½ cup freshly squeezed lime juice
1 tablespoons grated lime rind
¼ teaspoon salt
1¼ cups whipping cream, whipped
1 egg white
4 teaspoons superfine grind sugar

Preheat oven to 375°. Break graham crackers into quarters. In a food processor or blender, coarsely chop graham crackers. Spread the sugar and the butter slices evenly on top of the cracker crumbs in the processor or blender. Run the motor again for 15 to 20 seconds. Press mixture evenly into a 9-inch pie pan. Bake until crackly crisp, about 8 minutes. Cool to room temperature. With an electric mixer, beat the egg yolks until light yellow. Add the condensed milk; beat well. Add lime juice, rind and salt; beat well. Fold in 2 tablespoons of whipped cream. In a separate bowl, whip egg white with 4 teaspoons superfine sugar. Gently fold egg white into mixture keeping as much air as possible in mixture. Carefully spoon filling into crust; do not press down. Wrap the pie loosely in plastic wrap and freeze for 2 to 4 hours. Just before serving spread pie with remaining whipped cream.

Yield: 6 to 8 servings

MACAROON PIE

3 egg whites
1 teaspoon baking powder
1 cup sugar
¾ cup crushed soda crackers
1 cup dates
1 cup chopped nut meats
whipped cream to garnish

Beat egg whites until stiff, adding baking powder while beating eggs. Fold in sugar, 1 tablespoon at a time. Fold in crackers, then dates and nuts. Bake in greased pie tin in a 325° oven for 30 minutes. Serve with whipped cream.

Yield: 6 to 8 servings

AMARETTO PIE

1 (8-ounce) package
  softened cream cheese
1 (12-ounce) can
  evaporated milk
⅔ cup Amaretto liqueur

1 (16-ounce) container
  frozen whipped topping,
  thawed
5 ounces slivered almonds
2 graham cracker crusts

Cream together cream cheese, evaporated milk and liqueur. Fold whipped topping and almonds into creamed mixture. Pour into 2 prepared graham cracker crusts and garnish with additional almonds, if desired. If serving same day, chill for several hours in refrigerator or may be frozen up to 1 week ahead of use.

Yield: 8 to 12 servings

AVOCADO PIE

Crust:
1 (13-ounce) package
  crushed coconut
  macaroons

½ cup unsalted butter,
  melted

Filling:
2 eggs, separated
3 ripe avocados
  juice of 6 limes
1 teaspoon grated lime zest
½ cup sugar

1 cup sweetened condensed
  milk
  fresh slices of lime to
  garnish
  fresh strawberries to
  garnish

To make the crust, combine the crushed macaroons and melted butter in a bowl and stir to blend well. Press into a 10-inch pie pan and chill.

To make the filling, beat egg whites until stiff, but not dry; set aside. Purée the avocados in a food processor or blender. Add the lime juice, zest, sugar, condensed milk and egg yolks; blend until smooth. Fold in egg whites. Pour into chilled crust, wrap tightly in plastic wrap and freeze for at least 4 hours. To serve, thaw for about 15 minutes, then garnish with lime slices and/or strawberries.

Yield: 12 servings

ANGEL PIE

Pie Shell:

4	egg whites	1	teaspoon water
1	cup sugar	½	teaspoon baking powder
1	teaspoon vanilla extract	½	teaspoon salt
1	teaspoon vinegar		

Filling:

4	beaten egg yolks	1	tablespoon all-purpose
½	cup sugar		flour
1	lemon	½	cup water

Topping:

1	cup whipping cream	½	teaspoon vanilla extract

To prepare the pie shell, in a large mixing bowl, whip egg whites until they are stiff. Sift sugar into a separate bowl. In a separate cup, mix vanilla, vinegar and water. Add sifted sugar ½ teaspoon at a time to egg whites, alternating with a few drops of the combined liquids, beating well each time. When all the sugar and the liquid have been added, add baking powder and salt. Beat all ingredients until meringue is smooth. Pour into deep 10-inch buttered oven-proof pie plate. Bake in a 275° oven approximately 1 hour. Allow to cool in the oven with door open.

To make the filling, place egg yolks and sugar in top of double boiler. Juice the lemon and zest it. Place in double boiler with remaining ingredients. Cook over medium heat until thick, stirring constantly. Cool.

When pie shell and filling are cool, make topping by whipping together cream and vanilla. Place a layer of whipped cream in meringue shell, then a layer of filling, then another layer of whipped cream. Chill pie for several hours.

Yield: 6 servings

CHOCOLATE LACE COOKIES

1 pound unsalted butter, softened	3½ cups all-purpose flour
3 cups light brown sugar	1½ teaspoons salt
1 cup sugar	2 teaspoons baking soda
4 eggs	1 (12-ounce) package semi-sweet chocolate chips
2 teaspoons vanilla extract	

In a large mixing bowl, cream together butter and sugars. Beat in the eggs and vanilla extract. In a separate bowl, sift together flour, salt and baking soda; add to the creamed mixture. Melt the chocolate chips in the microwave or in the top of a double-boiler. Fold the melted chocolate chips into the creamed mixture. Drop dough by teaspoonfuls onto a greased cookie sheet. Bake in the top third of the oven at 375° for 8 to 10 minutes. Allow to cool on cookie sheet for 1 to 2 minutes. Remove with spatula. These cookies should be very thin and lacy around the edges with a candy-like texture. If they become too hard to remove from cookie sheet, return them to the oven for a minute to soften.

Yield: 5 to 6 dozen

CRUNCHY COOKIES

2 cups soft margarine	1 (7-ounce) can coconut
2 cups sugar	8 ounces white chocolate, cut into small chunks, (optional)
2 teaspoons vanilla	
3 cups all-purpose flour	
2 teaspoons cream of tartar	1½ cups macadamia nuts, coarsely chopped, (optional)
2 teaspoons baking soda	
2½ cups cornflakes	

Cream together margarine, sugar and vanilla. Add flour, cream of tartar and baking soda to creamed mixture. By hand, add 2½ cups cornflakes (do not crush) and coconut. If desired, fold in white chocolate and nuts. Drop by teaspoonful onto an ungreased cookie sheet. Bake at 350° for 10 to 12 minutes.

Yield: 5 dozen

RASPBERRY SANDIES

2½ cups all-purpose flour	1 egg, slightly beaten
1 cup sugar	¼ cup milk
1 teaspoon cinnamon	⅔ cup raspberry jam
¾ teaspoon baking powder	1 cup sifted powdered sugar
¼ teaspoon salt	¼ teaspoon vanilla extract
½ cup butter, softened	1½ tablespoons milk

Mix together flour, sugar, cinnamon, baking powder and salt. Make a well in the center, add butter, egg and milk and mix until moistened. Roll to ⅛-inch thickness. Chill dough and cut into 2-inch circles. Place on ungreased cookie sheet and bake in oven at 375° for 8 to 10 minutes. Let cool. Place ½ teaspoon jam on a cookie, place another cookie on top to make a "sandwich." Mix together powdered sugar, vanilla and milk until smooth to make a glaze. Spread cookies with glaze.

Yield: 50 cookies

PERSIMMON COOKIES

1 teaspoon baking soda	½ teaspoon salt
1 cup persimmon pulp	½ cup shortening
2 cups sifted all-purpose flour	1 cup sugar
	1 beaten egg
½ teaspoon cinnamon	1 cup chopped nuts
½ teaspoon cloves	1 cup raisins or chocolate chips
½ teaspoon nutmeg	

Dissolve baking soda in persimmon pulp and set aside. Sift together flour, cinnamon, cloves, nutmeg and salt. Cream together shortening and sugar. Add beaten egg to this mixture. Stir dry ingredients into persimmon mixture and add to egg mixture. Finally, add nuts and raisins or chocolate chips. Mix well. Drop by teaspoonful onto greased cookie sheet. Bake at 375° for 5 to 7 minutes.

Yield: 2 to 3 dozen

DATE COOKIES

1	cup shortening	1	cup dates, finely chopped
2	cups brown sugar	1	cup raisins
3	eggs	1	cup coconut
2¾	cups cake flour	½	cup chopped nuts
1	teaspoon baking soda	1	teaspoon vanilla
½	teaspoon salt		

Cream together shortening, brown sugar and eggs. Sift together cake flour, baking soda and salt. Add sifted ingredients to creamed ingredients and mix until smooth. Add remaining ingredients and mix well. Drop by teaspoonful, 2-inches apart, onto a greased cookie sheet. Bake at 375° for 10 to 12 minutes.

Yield: 3 to 4 dozen

OATMEAL PEANUT BUTTER COOKIES

1½	cups all-purpose flour	½	cup peanut butter
¼	teaspoon salt	2	eggs
½	teaspoon baking soda	1	teaspoon vanilla
1	teaspoon cinnamon	½	cup milk
4	tablespoons shortening	½	cup raisins
1	cup sugar	¾	cup oatmeal

Preheat oven to 350°. Sift together flour, salt, baking soda and cinnamon; set aside. Using a wooden spoon, in a large bowl, beat together shortening and sugar. Add peanut butter; blend together. In a small bowl, beat eggs and gradually add to peanut butter mixture. Slowly add vanilla, milk, sifted flour mixture, raisins and oatmeal. Cover and chill the dough for 1 hour. Drop by teaspoonful 2-inches apart onto cookie sheets. Bake until brown, about 12 minutes.

Yield: 3 to 4 dozen

GINGER SNAP COOKIES

¾ cup butter or margarine
1 cup sugar
1 egg
4 tablespoons molasses

2 cups sifted all-purpose
flour
1 teaspoon cinnamon
1 teaspoon ginger
2 teaspoons baking soda

Cream together shortening and sugar; add egg and beat until smooth. Add the molasses. Add cinnamon, ginger and baking soda to the flour and mix into the other ingredients. Shape dough into teaspoon-size balls, roll in sugar and place on a greased cookie sheet. Bake at 375° until crisp around the edges, about 5 to 10 minutes.

Yield: 2 to 3 dozen

AMISH SUGAR COOKIES

1 cup sugar
1 cup margarine, softened
2 beaten eggs
1 cup vegetable oil
2 teaspoons vanilla extract

1 cup powdered sugar
½ teaspoon salt
¾ teaspoon cream of tartar
4½ cups sifted flour

Preheat oven to 350°. In a large mixing bowl, cream together margarine and sugar. Add beaten eggs; stir. Add vegetable oil and vanilla extract; stir. In a separate bowl, combine powdered sugar, salt, cream of tartar and flour. Add dry ingredients to egg mixture and stir until well blended. Chill for about ½ hour. Lightly grease cookie sheet. Take tablespoon of chilled dough and roll into ball. Press gently with a glass that has been oiled on the bottom and dipped in sugar. Bake for about 10 minutes or until edges are lightly browned.

Yield: 3 dozen cookies

SCOTCH SHORTBREAD

½ cup butter, softened to
room temperature
⅓ cup powdered sugar

¼ teaspoon vanilla
(optional)
1 cup all-purpose flour

Cream together butter, sugar and vanilla. Gradually add flour and mix until dough is very smooth, kneading like bread dough, if necessary. Place the dough in the middle of an 8-inch square pan. Working out from the center, firmly press the dough into the pan. Prick the entire surface with a fork, and bake in a 325° oven for about 30 to 35 minutes or until lightly browned. Be sure that the middle is thoroughly baked. Allow to cool for 10 minutes. Cut into small squares while dough is still warm.

Yield: 64 1-inch squares

OATMEAL CHOCOLATE CHIP BROWNIES

1 cup semi-sweet chocolate
chips
⅓ cup butter or margarine
1 cup quick-cooking rolled
oats
¼ cup wheat germ
⅓ cup nonfat dry milk
½ teaspoon baking powder

½ cup chopped nuts
(optional)
2 eggs
1 teaspoon vanilla extract
¼ cup firmly packed light
brown sugar
2 tablespoons sugar

In heavy 2-quart saucepan or top of double-boiler, melt chocolate chips and butter over low heat and stir until fully mixed and smooth. Set aside to cool. In large mixing bowl, combine rolled oats, wheat germ, dry milk, baking powder and nuts. In separate medium-sized mixing bowl, beat eggs, vanilla and sugars until smooth; then add chocolate/butter mixture, stirring until smooth. Fold in the oats mixture until well blended. It will be very thick. Pour into a greased 8 x 8-inch pan. Bake in a 350° oven for 20 minutes. Cut into squares and serve.

Yield: 8 servings

FROSTED BROWNIES

Brownies:

3 squares unsweetened chocolate
¾ cup butter
1½ cups sugar
3 eggs
¾ cup flour
½ teaspoon salt
1½ teaspoons vanilla
¾ cup pecans (optional)

White Topping:

2¼ cups powdered sugar
½ cup butter
¾ cup whipping cream

Chocolate Topping:

3 squares unsweetened chocolate

To make the brownies, melt chocolate and butter in the top of a double boiler. Remove from heat and stir in sugar. Add eggs and beat well. Mix in flour and salt. Add vanilla and nuts. Pour into a well-buttered 13 x 9 x 2-inch pan. Bake in a 375° oven for 15 to 20 minutes. Cool.

To make the white topping, place powdered sugar, butter and whipping cream in a heavy saucepan. Heat over medium heat, stirring occasionally. When mixture holds together and coats the back of a metal spoon (soft-ball stage); remove from heat. Spread over cooled brownies. Allow white topping to cool.

To make the chocolate topping, melt chocolate in double boiler. Spread a thin layer over the white topping which has been allowed to cool. Cut into squares and serve.

Yield: 12 to 18 bars

BUTTERSCOTCH BROWNIES

½ cup margarine
2 cups brown sugar
2 eggs, beaten
2 teaspoons vanilla extract

1⅓ cups sifted all-purpose flour
2 teaspoons baking powder
1 cup chopped nuts (optional)

Melt margarine in saucepan. Add brown sugar, then beaten eggs; mix thoroughly with a wooden spoon. Add vanilla. Sift flour and baking powder into mixture; fold in nuts. Beat just until all the ingredients are thoroughly mixed. Pour into a slightly greased and floured 13 x 9 x 2-inch pan and bake at 325° for 25 to 30 minutes. Sprinkle powdered sugar on top and cut into squares when cool.

Yield: 12 to 18 bars

CHOCOLATE CARAMEL SQUARES

36 caramels
3 tablespoons evaporated milk or cream
3 tablespoons butter
¾ cup melted butter
1 cup flour

¾ cup brown sugar
1 cup oatmeal
¾ teaspoon salt
1 cup chocolate chips
½ cup chopped nuts (optional)

Preheat oven to 350°. In a double boiler, melt caramels with milk and 3 tablespoon butter. In a separate bowl, mix ¾ cup melted butter, flour, brown sugar, oatmeal and salt. Pat ¾ of the oatmeal mixture into a 13 x 9 x 2-inch pan. Bake 10 minutes. Pour caramel sauce over baked crust. Sprinkle remaining oatmeal mixture over top. Sprinkle chocolate chips and nuts on top. Bake 12 minutes. Cool. Cut into bars.

Yield: 12 to 18 bars

DATE BARS

3 eggs, unbeaten
1 cup sugar
2 tablespoons shortening, melted
1 cup dates, cut up
1 cup chopped walnuts

1 teaspoon baking powder
¼ teaspoon salt
5 tablespoons flour
powdered sugar to garnish

Add sugar to eggs; mix. Add shortening. Stir in dates and nuts. Sift together baking powder, salt and flour; stir into date mixture. Spread in an 8-inch square pan and bake 1 hour at 325°. When cool, cut into squares and dust with powdered sugar.

Yield: 16 2-inch squares

RASPBERRY SQUARES

1⅓ cups all-purpose flour
½ teaspoon baking soda
1 cup brown sugar
½ cup oatmeal

1 cup chopped nuts
½ cup margarine, melted
½ cup raspberry jam
¼ cup chopped raisins

Combine flour, baking soda, brown sugar, oatmeal, chopped nuts and margarine. Blend. Press ½ of the mixture into a lightly greased 11 x 7-inch pan. Spread with raspberry jam and chopped raisins. Sprinkle remaining mixture over the top. Bake at 350° for 30 minutes. Cool and cut into squares.

Yield: 8 to 10 bars

APRICOT HAZELNUT BARS

¼ cup Scotch whiskey	4 ounces semi-sweet chocolate, chopped, melted and cooled
2 teaspoons instant espresso powder	
¼ cup minced dried apricots	1 ounce unsweetened chocolate, chopped, melted and cooled
½ cup unsalted butter, softened	
½ cup firmly packed dark brown sugar	½ cup skinned toasted hazelnuts, chopped
¾ cup firmly packed light brown sugar	½ cup sifted all-purpose flour
2 large eggs	pinch of salt

Preheat oven to 350°. In a small bowl, whisk together whiskey and espresso powder. Add the apricots and let them marinate, covered, for 1 hour. Using an electric mixer, cream together butter and brown sugars. Beat in the eggs, one at a time, and chocolate. To toast and skin hazelnuts, place hazelnuts in a single layer on a baking sheet in a preheated 350° oven for 10 to 15 minutes, or until they are colored lightly and the skins blister. Wrap the nuts in a kitchen towel and let them steam for 1 minute. Rub the nuts in the towel to remove the skins and let them cool. Stir in apricot mixture, hazelnuts, flour, and a pinch of salt. Pour the batter into a well-buttered and floured 8-inch square baking pan and bake in the middle of oven for 35 to 40 minutes, or until a tester comes out with just a few crumbs clinging to it. Let cool completely and cut into bars.

Yield: 9 bars

KAHLUA PECAN BARS

1 pastry crust	3 eggs
¼ cup butter	½ cup Kahlua
¾ cup sugar	½ cup dark corn syrup
1 teaspoon vanilla extract	¾ cup evaporated milk
2 tablespoons all-purpose flour	1 cup chopped pecans

Line a 9 x 9-inch pan with your favorite pastry crust recipe. Chill. Preheat oven to 400°. Cream together butter, sugar, vanilla and flour. Mix well. Beat in eggs, one at a time. Stir in Kahlua, corn syrup, evaporated milk and pecans. Mix well; pour into pastry crust. Bake for 10 minutes, then reduce heat to 325° and bake until firm, about 40 minutes.

Yield: 1 dozen bars

SOUTHERN PECAN BARS

¼ cup butter	¾ cup dark corn syrup
⅓ cup brown sugar	¼ cup brown sugar
1 cup all-purpose flour	2 tablespoons all-purpose flour
¼ teaspoon baking powder	½ teaspoon salt
¼ cup chopped pecans	1 teaspoon vanilla extract
2 eggs	

Cream together butter and sugar. Blend flour and baking powder into butter mixture until it is like coarse meal; add pecans. Pat firmly into the bottom of a 9 x 9-inch ungreased pan. Bake at 350° for 10 minutes. Combine corn syrup, brown sugar, flour, salt and vanilla; pour over the cooked layer. Bake for another 25 minutes. Allow to cool. Cut into bars.

Yield: 16 bars

POACHED PEARS WITH MARSCAPONE
AND CARAMEL SAUCE

Filling:

½ cup Marscapone cheese

¼ cup powdered sugar

2 to 3 tablespoons rum or best brandy

Poached Pears:

2 lemons, juiced

1 cup water

4 large ripe but firm Bosc pears

⅓ cup granulated sugar

1 cup fruity white wine

zest of one lemon

1 vanilla bean, split

1 (3-inch) cinnamon stick

Caramel Sauce:

1 cup heavy cream

¼ cup sugar

1 cup water

¼ cup rum or brandy

3 tablespoons unsalted butter

fresh mint sprigs to garnish

To make the filling, mix together Marscapone cheese, powdered sugar and rum or brandy; whisk until well blended. Cover and refrigerate.

To prepare the pears, combine the lemon juice and water in a large bowl. Peel the pears as smoothly as possible, leaving stems intact and place in water mixture. Cut a slice off the bottom of each pear so they will stand upright. Core from the bottom, and place again in the lemon water to prevent discoloration. In a saucepan just large enough to hold all the pears upright, combine sugar, wine, lemon zest, vanilla bean and cinnamon stick. Bring to a boil, stirring to dissolve sugar. Fill the pear cavities with crumpled foil. Add the pears to boiling liquid, standing them upright, adding enough water to cover them. Reduce to a simmer, cover pan and poach until they are tender, but still hold their shape; approximately 10 to 20 minutes. With a slotted spoon, carefully remove pears to a shallow dish and cool. When cool, remove foil from cavities. Using a spoon or pastry bag, fill the pears with the cheese. Stand pears upright on a tray and chill until serving time.

Continued

Poached Pears with Marscapone and Caramel Sauce, continued

To make the sauce, scald the cream in a small heavy saucepan. Combine the sugar, water and rum in a small saucepan and cook, stirring until the mixture is a caramel color. Remove from the heat. While continuously stirring, slowly add hot cream and then butter. Keep the sauce warm or rewarm at serving time. To serve, place one pear on each dessert plate. Add additional dollop of Marscapone alongside the pear if desired. Slowly spoon warm sauce over the top of the pear. Garnish with a mint leaf.

Yield: 4 servings

PUMPKIN TORTE

1⅔ cups crushed vanilla wafers
⅓ cup brown sugar
½ cup melted butter
1 (8-ounce) package cream cheese
1 pound ricotta cheese
2 eggs
¾ cup sugar
1 (16-ounce) can pumpkin
3 egg yolks
½ cup sugar
½ cup milk
1 teaspoon ground cinnamon
1 teaspoon pumpkin spice
¼ teaspoon ground cloves
1 envelope unflavored gelatin
¼ cup cold water
3 egg whites
¼ cup sugar

Mix together crushed vanilla wafers, brown sugar and melted butter. Pat into a 13 x 9 x 2-inch pan. In separate bowl, mix together cream cheese, ricotta cheese, 2 eggs and ¾ cup sugar. Pour on top of crust in pan. Bake at 350° until cheese has settled, approximately 30 minutes. Cool. In medium saucepan, mix pumpkin, egg yolks, ½ cup sugar, milk, cinnamon, pumpkin spice and cloves. Heat over low flame stirring constantly until thickened, approximately 10 minutes. Cool. In a small bowl, dissolve gelatin in ¼ cup cold water. Blend dissolved gelatin into pumpkin mixture. In a separate bowl, mix egg whites and ¼ cup sugar. Beat with hand mixer on medium or high speed until fluffy. Fold into pumpkin mixture. Spread over cheese layer in pan. Refrigerate until firm.

Yield: 10 to 12 servings

FROZEN GRAND MARNIER SOUFFLÉ

6 egg yolks	¼ cup Grand Marnier
1 cup sugar	liqueur
2 tablespoons water	2½ cups whipping cream
1 tablespoon grated orange	cocoa to garnish
rind	

Place egg yolks in a large mixing bowl. Combine sugar, water and orange rind in heavy saucepan. Bring to a boil. Continue to boil slowly, for at least 2 minutes, swirling the saucepan from time to time to mix well. While mixing at high speed, slowly pour the sugar syrup into the egg yolks. Continue mixing at high speed until the volume has increased considerably and mixture is light and fluffy; add Grand Marnier. In a separate bowl, whip cream lightly and fold into egg mixture. Dessert can then be frozen in a covered container and served with an ice cream scoop or fit a paper collar around a soufflé dish and pour in the mixture and freeze in the soufflé dish. When ready to serve, remove the collar and sprinkle the top with cocoa.

Yield: 6 servings

PALMER HOUSE CHOCOLATE ICE CREAM

3 pounds dark bitter	1 gallon plus 3 quarts
chocolate	vanilla ice cream
4½ pounds sugar	1 ounce vanilla flavoring
1 gallon whipping cream	1 teaspoon salt

Combine chocolate, sugar and whipping cream; bring to a simmer. Add vanilla ice cream, vanilla flavoring and salt and place in an ice cream machine and freeze. Palmer House Chocolate Ice Cream has been served to almost every President in the 19th and 20th Centuries.

Yield: 4 gallons

CHARLOTTE RUSSE

4	teaspoons instant coffee	¼	cup cold water
½	cup dark rum		ice (for cooling custard)
6	large egg yolks	3	cups whipping cream
2	cups powdered sugar	16	lady fingers, split in half
¾	cup whole milk	12	small macaroon cookies
½	cup butter	1	(4-ounce) package
2	teaspoons vanilla extract		slivered almonds, toasted
2	teaspoons unflavored gelatin		

Dissolve instant coffee in rum. In a very large bowl, beat egg yolks. Slowly add powdered sugar to eggs. Mixture should be pale yellow and thick. In a small saucepan, warm milk, butter and vanilla until butter has melted. Slowly pour milk mixture into egg mixture, beating constantly. In a separate bowl, dissolve gelatin in cold water. Combine and blend dissolved gelatin with coffee/rum mixture. Add that to egg/milk mixture; blend thoroughly. Pour entire mixture into a large pan; heat very slowly over low heat. Stir constantly until mixture thickens into custard. DO NOT BOIL. Cool over a pot of ice. Beat whipping cream into stiff peaks. With rubber spatula, gently fold ⅔ of whipping cream into chilled custard mixture. Line springform pan with lady fingers, placing lady fingers on end. Pour ½ of custard mixture into pan. Crumble macaroons over custard. Pour remaining ½ of custard over macaroons. Freeze for 4 hours. Before serving, spread whipped cream onto frozen dessert as if frosting a cake. Sprinkle with toasted slivered almonds. Cut and serve immediately.

Yield: 8 servings

LEMON CURD

½ pound butter
4 cups sugar

6 eggs, beaten until frothy
5 large lemons, juiced

Melt butter and sugar in top of double boiler. Add beaten eggs and lemon juice. Cook on low to medium heat, stirring occasionally, until lemon curd is clarified, about ½ hour. Great with ginger snaps, as cake filler, on English muffins, or on fresh fruit. Great for gift giving. Will keep up to one month.

Yield: 5 (10-ounce) jars

BERRIES WITH ALMOND CREAM

¼ cup superfine sugar
2 teaspoons cornstarch
1½ cups milk
3 egg yolks, beaten
2 tablespoons Amaretto or
   ⅛ teaspoon almond
   extract

mixture of raspberries,
strawberries, and
blackberries, or other
berries of your choice

In a small heavy saucepan, combine sugar and cornstarch. Stir in milk; cook over medium heat stirring until thickened and bubbly. Cook 2 minutes more. Stir a little hot mixture into the yolks; return all to the saucepan; cook and stir until bubbly. Remove from heat and stir in the Amaretto or extract. Pour sauce into a medium bowl. Cover surface with clear plastic wrap to prevent skin from forming. Chill. Spoon the sauce over desired berries just before serving.

Yield: 4 servings

HOT WINED MELBA

¼ cup sugar
1 tablespoon cornstarch
1 (10-ounce) package
   frozen raspberries,
   thawed; reserve syrup

¾ (1-pound) can peach
   slices in heavy syrup,
   reserve ¼ cup syrup
½ cup port wine
1 tablespoon lemon juice
   vanilla ice cream

Combine sugar and cornstarch in saucepan. Add raspberry syrup, peach syrup and port. Add lemon juice; cook over medium heat, stirring until sauce is thick. Add raspberries. Just before serving, add peach slices. Spoon warm sauce over a scoop of vanilla ice cream.

Yield: 6 servings

SUMMER PEACHES

6 large ripe peaches
3 tablespoons sugar
⅓ cup peach brandy
8 ounces cream cheese

½ cup powdered sugar
1 cup whipping cream
2 cups fresh blueberries

Scald peaches in boiling water for 30 seconds and peel. Slice into ⅛'s into a bowl. Sprinkle with sugar and peach brandy. Chill for 4 hours. In a separate bowl, with electric mixer or wire whisk, beat cream cheese and powdered sugar until smooth. Whip cream and fold into cheese mixture; chill. Before serving, drain peaches, reserving the juice. Combine blueberries and peaches and fold into cream mixture. If too thick, add some of the reserved juice. Divide among six glass dishes and serve chilled.

Yield: 6 servings

CARAMEL APPLES

½ cup sugar
½ cup dark brown sugar
1 tablespoon cornstarch
½ cup whipping cream
½ cup butter

1 teaspoon vanilla extract
¼ cup chopped pecans (optional)
4 to 5 Granny Smith apples, cored and cubed

Combine sugars and cornstarch in medium saucepan. Gradually stir in cream. Add butter; cook over medium heat, stirring constantly. Bring to a boil and boil for 1 minute. Stir in vanilla and pecans. Allow to cool for 15 minutes. Place cubed apples in individual bowls. Pour sauce over each serving.

Yield: 6 servings

HOT CHOCOLATE PUDDING AND ICE CREAM SAUCE

Pudding:
3 squares bitter chocolate
1½ tablespoons butter
¾ cup sugar
2 eggs

1½ cups all-purpose flour
1½ teaspoons baking powder
¾ cup milk
1 teaspoon vanilla extract

Ice Cream Sauce:
1 cup whipping cream
1 egg
¾ cup sugar

⅓ cup butter, melted
⅛ teaspoon salt
1 teaspoon vanilla extract

To make the pudding, melt chocolate and butter in double boiler; add sugar. Mix all other ingredients together in a mixing bowl. Add to chocolate mixture. Put in a greased, covered, double boiler and steam for 2 hours. Do not lift lid during cooking time.

To make the ice cream sauce, whip cream in one bowl. In a separate bowl, beat egg. Add sugar and salt and beat again. Add melted butter and beat. Add vanilla and whipped cream.

Yield: 8 servings

HOT FUDGE SAUCE

½ cup butter
4 ounces unsweetened chocolate
3 cups sugar

1 (12-ounce) can evaporated milk
½ teaspoon salt
1 teaspoon vanilla extract

Melt butter in top of double boiler. Add chocolate and blend. Add sugar, milk, salt and vanilla and cook on low heat, stirring frequently for 20 minutes. Keep this topping in the refrigerator.

Yield: 1 quart

ENGLISH TOFFEE

1 cup butter or margarine
1 cup sugar
1 teaspoon vanilla extract
3 tablespoons water

2 or 3 large bars milk chocolate
½ cup coarsely chopped nuts (optional)

In a saucepan over low heat, slowly cook butter, sugar, vanilla and water, stirring constantly. In a separate pan, melt chocolate. Cover the bottom of a heavily buttered jelly roll pan with some of the melted chocolate. Let it harden. Add ¼ cup coarsely chopped nuts to toffee mixture, if desired. Pour over the chocolate. Allow to set. Spread more melted chocolate over the top. Sprinkle with remaining nuts before top layer of chocolate hardens. When all is cool, break into bite size pieces.

Yield: How hungry are you?

AMERICAN TOFFEE

1 pound milk chocolate
1 pound pecans
2½ cups brown sugar

1 pound butter
¼ teaspoon salt

Grind together chocolate and nuts. Spread ½ of mixture in a jelly roll pan. Over low heat, cook brown sugar, butter and salt to hard crack stage (310°). Immediately pour over the chocolate and nuts. Spread remaining nuts and chocolate on top. After toffee cools, break into serving size pieces.

Yield: Depends on how sweet your sweet tooth is!

LEMON FLUFF

4   egg yolks
½   cup sugar
4   tablespoons lemon juice

2   tablespoons water
½   pint whipping cream,
    whipped

Beat egg yolks until stiff. Add sugar, lemon juice and water. Cook in a double boiler, stirring until thick. Cool and add to ½ pint whipped cream, mixing well.

Yield: 8 servings

RHUBARB COMPOTE

1   pound rhubarb
    sugar to taste
¼   cup raspberries

¼   cup shredded almonds,
    lightly toasted

Cut rhubarb into 1-inch chunks and cook, 1 cup at a time, in boiling water for about 2 minutes or until chunks rise to the surface of the water. By cooking the rhubarb 1 cup at a time, it stays chunky, pink and juicy and does not become soggy. As each batch is done, remove with a slotted spoon and place in a bowl, sprinkling with sugar to taste. Cooked rhubarb tends to taste sour when hot, so be careful not to over-sweeten. Let compote cool and taste to see if more sugar is needed. Refrigerate. Serve rhubarb in individual bowls and place a tablespoon of raspberries in the center of each serving. Sprinkle with toasted almonds.

Yield: 4 servings

FIREHOUSE FAVORITES

Hook and ladder companies were an
important part of the firefighting effort.

FIREHOUSE FAVORITES

The men and women firefighters from Chicago and its suburbs do not only fight fires; they are also talented and creative cooks.

The tasty recipes found in **FIREHOUSE FAVORITES** were contributed by the members of fire departments from the Villages of Northfield, Wilmette and Winnetka and from a fire department in Chicago, Engine Company #98, Ambulance #11 located near the Water Tower. We thank them for their help!

DOMINGO SCRAMBLED OMELETTE

2 sticks Chorizo sausage,
  skinned
3 tablespoons butter
2 onions, chopped
2 bell peppers (red and
  green), chopped
1 clove garlic, chopped
2 dozen eggs

4 ounces half-and-half
1 teaspoon sugar
  dash vanilla extract
  salt and pepper to taste
  salsa and/or grated
  Cheddar cheese
  (optional)

In a small skillet, cook fat from sausage. Remove meat and transfer to a large skillet. Melt butter and sauté onions, peppers, garlic and sausage. In a large bowl, whip eggs, half-and-half, sugar and vanilla. When vegetables are translucent, pour in eggs. Scramble over a low flame. When eggs are done, salt and pepper to taste. Before serving, garnish with grated Cheddar cheese and/or salsa if desired.

Yield: 10 servings

PORK RIBS AND SAUERKRAUT

2 (1-pound) cans
  sauerkraut
2 cups chopped onion
2 (28-ounce) cans
  tomatoes, crushed

1½ cups brown sugar
5 to 6 pounds country-style
  pork ribs

Layer ingredients in a large casserole dish or roaster pan in the order listed, starting with sauerkraut and ending with ribs. Do not stir. Cover and bake at 325° for 3 hours. Uncover for the last 45 minutes of baking time.

Yield: 8 to 10 servings

PORK ROAST

1 (6-pound) boneless pork loin roast, rolled and tied	1 onion
1 tablespoon Cajun spice	3 (16-ounce) cans potatoes
1 teaspoon garlic powder	4 tablespoons barbecue sauce
2 tablespoons cider vinegar	2 tablespoons brown sugar
2 tablespoons soy sauce	cornstarch

Put meat in a large roasting pan. Sprinkle with Cajun spice, garlic, vinegar and soy sauce. Sliver onions and spread around roast. Open and drain canned potatoes; place around roast. If needed, add a little water or broth so potatoes are half submerged. Place in oven and bake 25 to 30 minutes per pound at 325°. Baste roast and potatoes every hour. During the final 25 minutes, spread the top of roast with barbecue sauce. Remove roast from pan when done. Cool. Place oven pan on top of stove. Heat gravy and potatoes; thicken with cornstarch and brown sugar. Serve roast with gravy and potatoes.

Yield: 10 servings

TERIYAKI CHICKEN BREASTS

7 boneless skinless chicken breasts
1 (12-ounce) bottle teriyaki sauce
1 lime, juiced
2 tablespoons cooking oil
2 cloves garlic, chopped
2 onions, sliced
2 green peppers, sliced
1 teaspoon sesame seeds
2 tablespoons soy sauce
1 (7-ounce) can bamboo shoots
1 tablespoon cornstarch
1 tablespoon sugar
   white pepper
4 scallions, sliced

Halve and trim breasts. Marinate in teriyaki sauce and lime juice for 30 minutes. Heat oil in a large skillet; cook garlic for 5 minutes. Add chicken reserving ½ to ¾ cup marinade. Place sliced onion on top of cooking chicken. Add green pepper, sesame seeds, soy sauce and bamboo shoots; simmer. Mix reserved marinade, cornstarch and sugar. Pour on top of simmering chicken and continue to cook until thickened. Season to taste with white pepper. Garnish with scallions. Serve over rice.

Yield: 10 servings

CHEESE GLAZED CHICKEN BREASTS

3 to 4 whole chicken
   breasts, split and skinned
½ cup all-purpose flour
2 teaspoons paprika
2 teaspoons seasoned salt
2 tablespoons butter
2 tablespoons vegetable oil
⅓ cup dry sherry

1 cup half-and-half
1 tablespoon all-purpose
   flour
½ teaspoon salt
½ cup dry white wine
1 tablespoon lemon juice
4 to 6 ounces grated Swiss
   cheese

Mix ½ cup flour, paprika and seasoned salt in a large plastic bag. Coat the chicken by shaking several pieces at a time in the bag. Heat butter and oil in large skillet over medium heat; add chicken and brown on both sides. Add sherry; cook, uncovered, until chicken is just done, about 25 minutes. Remove chicken from pan with slotted spoon; keep warm. In a separate bowl, mix half-and-half, 1 tablespoon flour, and ½ teaspoon salt until smooth. Add this to pan drippings. Cook and stir over medium heat until slightly thickened, about 10 minutes. Add wine and lemon juice; heat through. Return chicken to pan; top with cheese. Cover and cook over low heat until cheese melts, about 2 minutes. Serve with rice. or noodles.

Yield: 8 servings

GRILLED TURKEY WITH STUFFING

1 (15-pound) turkey
1 (24-ounce) loaf white
   bread
1 large onion, chopped
5 celery ribs with leaves,
   chopped
3 cloves garlic, minced

3 eggs
1 tablespoon poultry
   seasoning
½ to 1 cup chicken broth
½ cup vegetable oil
1 (5-pound) bag charcoal
   briquettes

Arrange 40 charcoal briquettes on 2 sides of a drip pan set into a grill. Ignite coals and let burn for about 30 minutes or until white ash forms. Prepare stuffing by tearing up bread into 1-inch cubes. Add celery, onion and garlic. Mix with eggs and poultry seasoning. Add enough broth to achieve desired moistness. Stuff turkey cavity; rub oil on bird. Grill over drip pan making sure to add 5 coals per side, per hour. Baste occasionally with remaining chicken broth. A 15-pound turkey will take approximately 5 to 5½ hours to cook or when meat thermometer registers 185° when inserted in the thickest part of the thigh, not touching the bone. Allow to sit on carving board 20 minutes before carving.

Yield: 8 to 10 servings

BRACCIOLES WITH ITALIAN GRAVY

Braccioles:

3 pounds flank steak
1 cup bread crumbs
2 hard-boiled eggs, chopped
  salt and pepper to taste

oregano to taste
2 tablespoons vegetable or olive oil

Italian Gravy:

1 (8-ounce) can tomato sauce
1 (3-ounce) can tomato paste, mixed with 2 cans water

salt and pepper to taste
oregano to taste
1 tablespoon dried parsley
⅛ cup sugar

To prepare braccioles, pound flank steak flat. In a separate bowl, mix remaining ingredients. Spread mixture on top of steak and roll up in jelly-roll fashion. Tie the meat up with twine to hold it together. Brown meat in oil. Cook in Italian gravy over low heat for 2 to 2½ hours.

To make gravy, place all ingredients in a 3-quart saucepan and bring to a boil. Reduce to low heat and simmer for 45 minutes. Halfway through cooking, add sugar. Pour sauce over braccioles when done cooking. Serve with your choice of pasta, garlic bread and salad.

Yield: 6 servings

SPAGHETTI SAUCE

8 cloves garlic, chopped
2 large onions, chopped
1 large green pepper, chopped
1 pound mushrooms, chopped
2 tablespoons olive oil
4 pounds ground beef
1½ pounds Italian sausage
2 (16-ounce) cans Italian tomatoes
1 tablespoon bitters
2½ tablespoons salt

1 teaspoon black pepper
1 teaspoon celery salt
½ teaspoon cayenne pepper
1 tablespoon dried basil
1½ tablespoons Worcestershire sauce
2 tablespoons sugar
3 bay leaves
1 tablespoon dried oregano
1 (12-ounce) can tomato paste
1 (16-ounce) can tomato sauce

Sauté garlic, onions, green pepper and mushrooms in olive oil until soft. Place in a large stock pot. In a separate skillet, brown ground beef and sausage; drain and place in stock pot. Add remaining ingredients and cook over low heat for 4 hours.

Yield: 10 servings

BEEF STROGANOFF

2 tablespoons vegetable oil
4 pounds beef tenderloin, cut into strips
3 large onions, sliced
1 pound mushrooms
1 teaspoon Worcestershire sauce
2 (13¾-ounce) cans beef broth
2 tablespoons ketchup
1 cup cooking sherry
1 cup water
1 cup sour cream
salt and pepper to taste
chopped parsley to garnish

In a large skillet, brown beef in oil. Remove with a slotted spoon; place in a 3-quart saucepan. Sauté onions in same skillet and transfer to saucepan along with meat. Add remaining ingredients except sour cream, parsley and salt and pepper. Cook over low heat for 1 hour. Season with salt and pepper to taste. Just before serving, add the sour cream and adjust seasonings if necessary. Serve over noodles and sprinkle with fresh chopped parsley.

Yield: 8 to 10 servings

SHRIMP TETRAZZINI

1 (8-ounce) package fettuccine
2 tablespoons butter
1 medium onion, chopped
8 ounces shrimp
8 ounces fresh mushrooms, sliced
¼ cup all-purpose flour
¼ cup mayonnaise
1 teaspoon salt
2 cups milk
¼ cup dry sherry
Parmesan cheese

Cook fettuccine according to package directions; drain and set aside. Melt butter in skillet and sauté onion until tender. Add shrimp and mushrooms. Cook for 5 minutes, stirring often. Remove from skillet. Place flour, mayonnaise, salt, milk and sherry in skillet and cook over low heat until thickened. Toss with shrimp and fettuccine and turn into a 1½-quart casserole dish. Top with grated Parmesan cheese. Bake at 350° for 30 minutes.

Yield: 4 to 6 servings

SEAFOOD CHOWDER

2 tablespoons butter
2 medium onions, chopped
2 carrots, chopped
4 potatoes, peeled and cubed
2 ribs celery, chopped
12 ounces frozen corn (optional)
12 ounces fresh mushrooms (optional)
2 (6.5-ounce) cans minced clams
1 (8-ounce) bottle clam juice

2 quarts milk
15 mussels, washed and beards removed
2 pounds shelled shrimp
1 pound scallops
2 pints whipping cream
2 to 3 tablespoons cornstarch
garlic powder
salt and pepper to taste
chopped scallions to garnish

In a large stock pot, melt butter and add onions, carrots, potatoes and celery. Sauté until onions and celery are translucent. If using corn and/or mushrooms, add them to pot now. Add clams and clam juice. Simmer 5 minutes. Add milk; simmer but do not boil or scald. Add mussels, shrimp and scallops; stir. Add cream and simmer 5 minutes. Season with garlic powder, salt and pepper to taste. Garnish with chopped scallions.

Yield: 20 servings

GLAZED CARROTS

1 (1-pound) bag carrots, peeled and cut
water
2 tablespoons butter
1 tablespoon maple syrup

1 teaspoon ground mustard
½ teaspoon coarse ground black pepper
1 tablespoon parsley
salt

In a 2-quart saucepan, cover carrots with water and simmer for 20 minutes. Drain water when tender. Add butter, syrup, mustard, pepper and parsley. Stir until evenly glazed. Salt to taste.

Yield: 4 servings

PASTA SALAD

1 (16-ounce) package tri-color rotini
2 cloves garlic, minced
1 teaspoon salt
¼ cup olive oil
¼ cup red wine vinegar
½ teaspoon black pepper
2 teaspoons dried basil
½ teaspoon dried oregano
½ teaspoon dried rosemary
2 tablespoons diced green onion
2 tomatoes, diced
½ pound mozzarella cheese, cubed
1 red pepper, diced
1 yellow pepper, diced
1 (3-ounce) can diced black olives
½ pound diced salami

Cook pasta according to package directions. Rinse in cold water and drain; place in a large salad bowl. Add garlic, salt and pepper; mix well. Add oil, vinegar and spices; mix well. Add remaining ingredients, cover and allow to sit for at least 2 hours. Adjust seasonings to taste. Serve cold.

Yield: 6 servings

TACO SALAD

1 head iceberg lettuce
1 medium purple onion
2 pounds ground beef
2 medium tomatoes, diced
1 (3-ounce) can diced black olives
1 (16-ounce) package shredded Cheddar cheese
1 (8-ounce) bottle French salad dressing
2 tablespoons salsa hot pepper sauce to taste
1 (16-ounce) can kidney beans
1 (16-ounce) large bag tostada chips

Brown ground beef; drain and cool. Roughly chop lettuce and onions. Place in a large salad bowl. Add ground beef, kidney beans, tomatoes, olives and cheese. Mix well. Toss with ½ bottle of salad dressing, salsa and hot pepper sauce. Serve with crushed tostada chips on top.

Yield: 6 servings

SPLIT PEA AND HAM SOUP

1	ham shank bone with lots of meat	1	teaspoon dried thyme
	water to cover ham bone by 2 inches	2	cups chopped celery, tops included
1½	pounds dry green split peas	2	cups chopped carrots
		3	cups chopped onion
3	bay leaves	3	cloves garlic, minced
			salt and pepper to taste

Boil ham bone and skim off fat as it rises to the surface. Reduce to simmer and add split peas. Continue to simmer for 1½ hours, stirring occasionally until smooth. Remove ham bone and let it stand until cool enough to handle. While bone is cooling, add remaining ingredients and simmer until carrots and celery are tender, about 30 to 45 minutes. Pick meat off bone in 1-inch chunks and return to soup.

Yield: 8 servings

CHERNOBLE CHILI

4	pounds ground beef	1½	teaspoons paprika
3	(12-ounce) cans Rotel tomatoes	1	tablespoon crushed red pepper
2	medium onions, coarsely chopped	2	teaspoons cayenne pepper
1	fresh jalapeño pepper, finely chopped	1½	teaspoons cumin
4	(16-ounce) cans hot chili beans	1½	tablespoons chili powder
1	clove garlic, finely chopped		chopped onions to garnish grated Cheddar cheese to garnish

Brown beef and drain. In a very heavy duty cast iron pot, add the rest of ingredients to the beef. Cook over low heat for approximately 4 hours. Stir with a wooden spoon and stand back, fumes may be hazardous to your health! Serve with chopped onion and Cheddar cheese.

Yield: 10 brave souls

SCALLOPED POTATOES

2	pounds potatoes	2½	cups milk
¼	cup diced onion	3	tablespoons flour
1	teaspoon salt	1	(16-ounce) package
¼	teaspoon black pepper		grated Cheddar cheese
¼	cup butter		

Slice potatoes and place in a 2-quart glass baking dish with onions. Season with salt and pepper. In a separate bowl, mix milk and flour; pour over potatoes. Cover and bake at 350° for ½ hour then uncover and continue baking for 50 minutes longer. Sprinkle Cheddar cheese on potatoes and bake for 10 minutes more.

Yield: 6 servings

NECTARINE COBBLER

7	ripe nectarines	2	cups dry biscuit mix
1	lemon or lime	1	tablespoon vanilla or
2	cups sugar		lemon extract
3	teaspoons cornstarch	3	eggs
8	tablespoons butter, melted	½	cup brown sugar

Slice nectarines into wedges. Place in a mixing bowl. Squeeze lemon or lime over nectarines; add 1 cup sugar and cornstarch. Mix so that nectarines are well glazed. Place in a well buttered 13 x 9 x 2-inch baking dish. In a separate mixing bowl, blend melted butter, biscuit mix, 1 cup sugar, extract and eggs, mixing well. Drizzle over top of nectarines. Sprinkle top with brown sugar. Bake for 35 minutes at 350° or until golden brown. Serve with vanilla ice cream.

Yield: 10 servings

HOLY COW, CHICAGO'S COOKING! offers

a wide range of recipes for good eating from a diverse group of Chicago area cooks. This book has been a three year project for the following:

COOKBOOK COMMITTEE

Chairman	Cindy Stuhley
Co-Chairman	Bobbie Vender
Treasurer	Carol Lockwood
Testing	Heidi Campbell
	Carolyn Cartwright
	Barbara Haljun
	Barbara Paine
Production	Cheryl Anderson
	Phyllis Shelton
Design	Courtney Boyd Davis
Illustration	Gretchen Grant
Marketing	Barbara Breuer
	Heidi Mangel
Storyline	Arden Frederick
	Jacqueline Thompson
Editing	Eleanor Johnston
	Linda Relias
Word Processing	Heidi Campbell
	Ann Horstmann
	Lorraine Patin
	Cindy Stuhley

...and the efforts of all members of each committee.

A special thanks to the following people for support and inspiration:

The Reverend Robert K. Myers, Ph.D.

Heidi Mangel	Russell Bennett	Nancy True
Anne Curti	Harriet Young	Carol McCall
Mary Frances Witte	Richard Wood	Sue Stanfa
Huey Company	Lynda Harrill	Susan Heath

The Winnetka Fire Department
The Northfield Fire Department
The Wilmette Fire Department
The Chicago Fire Department, Engine #98, Ambulance # 11

Our sincere thanks and appreciation to the families and friends of the Church of the Holy Comforter who contributed recipes. We truly hope no one has been inadvertently omitted.

Ellen Abell
Mary Air
Marge Allyn
Polly Allyn
Cheryl Anderson
Leslie Baker
*Kevin Barry
Virginia Becker
Patty Bennett
Cindy Berlinghof
Irene Bower
Mary Bradbury
Barbara Breuer
John Breuer
Ruth Bromley
Bob Buenger
Trudy Bunge
Georgia Burnett
June Callies
Heidi Campbell
Margaret Campbell
Ruth Carlson
Joan Carter
Carolyn Cartwright
Sandy Chelius
Betty Cittadine
Bonnie Clark
Irene Coles
Jane Coley
Lynn Collins
Allison Condit
Trudy Cook
Cissy Crawford
Martha Cray
Barbara Croft
Anne Curti
Gladys Danforth
Courtney Davis
Mary Lou Deakyne
Marjorie Dennis
Annette Denunzio
Molly DePatie
Barb Devlin
Alison Dienner
Joan Dodson
Janet Drake
Melissa Drake
Carrie Drew

Blanche Dryud
Joyce Evans
Marjorie Fairman
Mary Fields
Nancy
    Ford-Murphy
Arden Frederick
*Darlene Frost
*Mike Frost
Catherine Garnett
Kate Gilbertson
*Karl Graff
Sarah Grauer
Marilyn Greable
Marilyn Gunn
Barbara Haljun
Rose Hanner
Betsy Hartman
Susan Heath
Christine
    Heatherington
Priscilla Hecht
Blanche
    Heidengren
Kay Henderson
LaVere Hess
Anne Heynen
Mark Higgins
Ruth Hillsman
Mary Hoffmann
Ann Horstmann
Stepheny Houghtlin
Inger Hughson
Liz Hupp
Cindy Ilg
Nancy Jackson
Candy Jefcoat
Ruth Jenness
Eleanor Johnston
Jean Jones
Liz Jones
Mary Jones
Suzy Jones
Mary Juers
Barbara Kehoe
Penny Kezios
Mildred Klatte
*Jeff Klauke

Pam Lane
Jody Lapp
Betty Larsen
Sophie Laser
Connie Layton
Mary Laun
*Steve Laureys
*Jim LaVigne
Diane Levy
Nancy Lindner
Carol Lisle
Carol Lockwood
Karen Longo
Adrienne Lower
Barbara Lucyshyn
Eleanor
    MacCracken
Jean MacDonald
*Sharon Mahoney
Heidi Mangel
John Mangel
Judy Marquardt
Isabelle Martin
*Dick May
Carol McCall
Beryl McCleary
Suzy Mead
Nancy
    Melsheimer
Eugenie Mikhael
Olga Moore
Onnie Morgan
Dottie Morley
Mary Jane Morley
Jill Mueller
Florrie Munat
Bonnie Myers
Corine Myers
Cathy Nicholson
Marilyn Norehad
Roslyn O'Connor
Carol Olson
Pam Page
Barbara Paine
Marian Peterson
Fran Powell
Sara Lee Powell
Gretchen Quinn

Betsy Ramsdell
Lee Rapach
Judy Reed
Linda Relias
Carolyn Rohlen
Sue Rossiter
Barbara Rothrock
Molly Sale
Joanne Schildberg
Ted Schurch
Phyllis Shelton
Nina Slootmaker
Judy Smart
Cathy Smid
*James Staatz
Olga Stokes
Nancy Stuart
Cindy Stuhley
Janice Suddath
Katie Synek
Barbranell
    Taubensee
Harriett Taylor
Anne Teeple
Liz Thomas
Jacqueline
    Thompson
Georgia Thurman
Mary Todd
Sue Toth
Nancy True
Judy Urban
Bobbie Vender
*Al Vilches
Emily Voit
Barbara Waiting
Joan Webber
Barbara Weinberger
Barbara Whiting
Cynthia Whybrow
Anne Williams
Lloyd Williams
Yvonne Williams
Pat Windhorst
Marjorie Wolf
Harriet Young
    *Contributing
        Firefighters

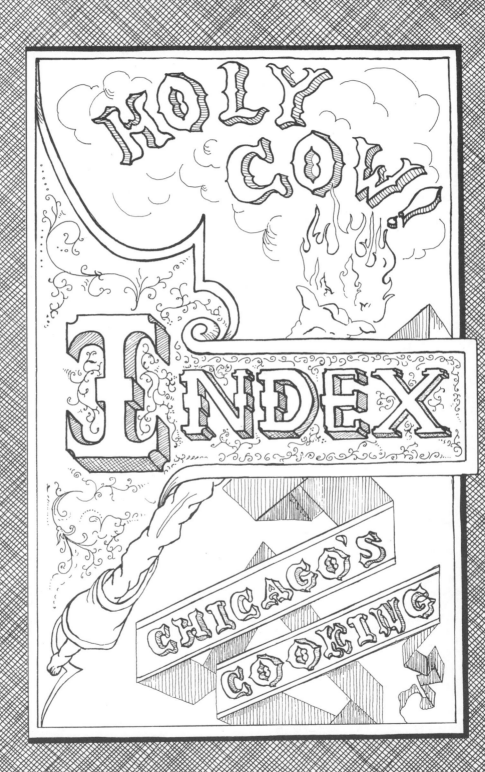

HOLY COW, CHICAGO'S COOKING !
P.O. Box 168, Kenilworth, IL 60043

Please send _____ copy(ies)   @ $16.95 each   _____
Ill res.add 7.75% sales tax   _____
Postage & handling   @ $3.25 each   _____
                                          total _____

Send to:
Name _____
Address: _____
City _____ State _____ Zip _____

Please make checks payable to: Women of the Church of the Holy Comforter.

--- --- --- --- --- --- --- --- --- --- --- --- --- --- --- --- --- ---

HOLY COW, CHICAGO'S COOKING !
P.O. Box 168, Kenilworth, IL 60043

Please send _____ copy(ies)   @ $16.95 each   _____
Ill res.add 7.75% sales tax   _____
Postage & handling   @ $3.25 each   _____
                                          total _____

Send to:
Name _____
Address: _____
City _____ State _____ Zip _____

Please make checks payable to: Women of the Church of the Holy Comforter.

--- --- --- --- --- --- --- --- --- --- --- --- --- --- --- --- --- ---

HOLY COW, CHICAGO'S COOKING !
P.O. Box 168, Kenilworth, IL 60043

Please send _____ copy(ies)   @ $16.95 each   _____
Ill res.add 7.75% sales tax   _____
Postage & handling   @ $3.25 each   _____
                                          total _____

Send to:
Name _____
Address: _____
City _____ State _____ Zip _____

Please make checks payable to: Women of the Church of the Holy Comforter.